No Time to
Say Goodbye

No Time to Say Goodbye

Surviving the suicide
of a loved one

CARLA FINE

D o u b l e d a y

New York   London   Toronto   Sydney   Auckland

PUBLISHED BY DOUBLEDAY
a division of Bantam Doubleday Dell Publishing Group, Inc.
1540 Broadway, New York, New York 10036

DOUBLEDAY and the portrayal of an anchor with a dolphin are
trademarks of Doubleday, a division of Bantam Doubleday Dell
Publishing Group, Inc.

Library of Congress Cataloging-in-Publication Data

Fine, Carla.
No time to say goodbye: surviving the suicide of a loved one /
Carla Fine. — 1st ed.
p.   cm.
Includes bibliographical references (p.   ).
1. Suicide—Psychological aspects.   2. Bereavement—
Psychological aspects.   3. Suicide victims—Family relationships.
I. Title.
HV6545.F525   1997
362.28'3—dc20   96-8388
CIP

ISBN 0-385-48018-0

Book design by Richard Oriolo

Printed in the United States of America

January 1997

First Edition

1 2 3 4 5 6 7 8 9 10

To Alex,
For being there—then and always

Acknowledgments

The courage and strength of the many people who shared the intimate, often painful details of the suicide of their loved ones for this book will remain with me always. I am grateful for their confidence that in my telling of their experiences, the stigma surrounding suicide will begin to diminish through understanding and compassion.

In every survivor's journey, there are sources of comfort and direction that help to ease the anguish and clear the confusion. I would especially like to thank my mother, Lillian Fine, for her love and unwavering support, and my sisters, Jill, Janet, and Ellen, for showing me the true definition of family. I would also like to thank my "hermana," Dolly Velasco, for her passionate faith in the triumph of the creative spirit in the face of adversity and fear.

A survivor remembers every kindness extended during a time when the world seems suddenly threatening and unfamiliar. I am grateful for the consideration given to me by Patricia Hennessey, Marie Stareck, Doreen Liebeskind, Phil Fierro, Jean-Claude Deshauteurs, Peter Klausner, and Jeffrey Schwartz. I am also in debt to Debby Glazer for her humanistic insight and steadfast presence, and to Elaine Frances for her conviction in my ability to flourish with change.

This book exists today as a result of the determination of my agent and friend, Barbara Lowenstein, who trusted in its worth from the beginning, and my editor, Judy Kern, who championed its cause and helped me communicate its message as clearly as possible. I truly appreciate their warm encouragement and belief in my work. I am also grateful to Mary Mooney for her keen intellect and astute suggestions, and to Edward Dunne for his enlightened counsel and thoughtful input.

Out of the ashes of tragedy, unexpected gifts often emerge. I will always cherish the friendship of Sonia and Ron Heuer, with whom I have spent endless hours baring my soul yet instinctively connect without the necessity of words, and to Gerry Graffe for her generous heart and wonderful gift of knowing how to laugh. I am also honored by my friendship with Suzi Epstein, a wise and courageous woman, and with Aukia Betancourt, whose future knows no bounds.

I am especially indebted to Ilka Tanya Payan, who in her fierce struggle against the terrible plague of AIDS taught me about the beauty and dignity of the human spirit. I am also grateful to Pam Parlapiano, Vicki Ciampa, and Maxine Gold for their humor and loyal support.

Most important, I would like to thank Alex Kopelman, my eternal soulmate, who has been with me through every step of this odyssey. A fine writer who helped shape the tone and direction of this book, Alex's vision and faith in me have never wavered. And, of course, I must not forget Cinco, who reminded me that there was joy even in my deepest darkness and who never left my side.

Finally, I would like to pay tribute to my husband, Harry Reiss, and the memories of others whose lives have been ended by an unrelenting despair and sadness that only they could know. It is my hope that their stories will provide some kind of insight for those of us who are left behind, ensuring that their deaths will not have been in vain.

Contents

Contents

No Time to
Say Goodbye

Part One

INTRODUCTION

Letting Go of
the Silence

It was the first warm day after a particularly cold and brutal winter. As the bus maneuvered its way through the midtown traffic, I stared out the window at the office workers enjoying the sunshine on their lunchtime break. I recognized him immediately, striding decisively among the slower-walking pedestrians. His expensive gray suit was similar to the one he had worn to the monthly meetings. He was carrying the same brown leather briefcase—I could picture how he would set it upright by his side as soon as he sat down, its very presence proclaiming order and routine in the middle of our circle of chaos.

He prided himself on his resolve. "I am getting on with my life," he would announce to the rest of us, his grief-clouded eyes betraying his words. "Things are settling back to normal and I've started moving forward," he would repeat, as if having memorized a speech someone else had written for him.

This ordinary-looking businessman and I had been brought together years before by a shared anguish: the suicide of someone we loved. Twice a month, for more than a year, we met with five or ten or twenty other strangers in the basement of a church, trying to make some sense of our unthinkable tragedies, hoping to feel less alone with our feelings of craziness and disorientation. We walked into those meetings rudderless, not knowing what had hit us. We were survivors of a shipwreck, consumed by guilt for having failed to save the dearest people in our lives and ashamed at being alive and abandoned. We were dazed by our helplessness, confused by the anger that laced through our mourning.

He quickly disappeared into the noonday crowd, merging into the steady stream of people filling the vibrant street. I wished I could have spoken to him, to find out how he had fared over these past years. Had he truly been able to put his life back together after the piercing horror of his daughter's suicide? Was he still married? Did he reconcile with his son? Had the nightmare of finding his daughter's motionless body in a blood-filled bathtub dimmed enough to allow him some moments of peace? Had he forgiven himself?

And what about me? I looked at the spindly trees lining the avenue, their buds bravely welcoming another year of urban hazards. I thought about the flowers planted near Harry's grave in a small Massachusetts cemetery. Were they also beginning to bloom? I wondered. Had they survived the fierce ice storms and snow blasts of these past months?

On December 16, 1989, my husband had been unable to survive a similarly harsh winter, killing himself in the waning light of a late Saturday afternoon. My once-familiar world exploded with his suicide; in an instant, the life we had built together during our marriage of twenty-one years ended, without discussion or time for goodbyes.

I remembered the bus ride I took to my first meeting of the support group, one month after Harry's suicide. It was January 12, 1990, Harry's forty-fourth birthday. I felt as if I had not slept since the moment I discovered him dead in his medical office, the intravenous tube that delivered a lethal dose of Thiopental, a powerful anesthetic, still attached to the crook of his arm. The horrific events of that past month were like a dream; nothing seemed quite real to me. I was unable to cry, as if my tears would somehow confirm that he was really gone.

I had found him lying on his examining table, covered with blood. The room was a mess. Empty bottles of Thiopental were strewn on the floor, along with discarded needle packets, plastic tubing, and several Milky Way wrappers. The IV pole was upright, tethered to Harry's waist by his black leather belt.

Harry was wearing his favorite pink shirt, with both sleeves rolled up. Draped around his neck was the green woolen scarf his mother in Colombia had knitted for him to use during the cold New York winters; he had treasured the scarf most among all his possessions, considering it a talisman that would protect him against unforeseen dangers.

Both the shirt and the scarf were soaked with blood. For days afterward, I obsessed about the blood. It was as if, by solving the riddle of his blood, I would somehow be able to understand the logic of his suicide. Did he try to pull the IV tube out of his arm at the last minute and rip an artery? Had an intruder knocked him on the head and arranged his death to look like a suicide? Had he somehow managed to shoot himself after he injected the Thiopental? I finally found the courage to telephone the medical examiner, who told me that blood had leaked from Harry's nose and mouth as a result of an anticoagulant he had taken so his veins would not become blocked and impede the flow of the Thiopental. "As a physician, your husband had it all figured out," he said. The medical examiner's tone conveyed his professional admiration, as if the logic of Harry's actions was more a testimonial to his medical acumen than a terrifying window into his desperate state of mind.

The medical examiner also told me that it had been an extremely peaceful death. "He was asleep in seconds, dead in minutes," he estimated, adding that this was the first death from Thiopental he had seen in New York City. "The drug is used as a pre-anesthetic, to sedate patients before surgery," he explained. "Your husband didn't suffer, if that's any comfort."

There would be no comfort. I knew this as soon as I discovered the gruesome scene in Harry's office. How could he have left me like this? Why hadn't he turned to me for help? What if I had come to his office an hour earlier? Why did I allow him to convince me that he didn't need professional counseling for his growing depression after the deaths of his mother and father in the past year? What if I had been more insistent about our going out to dinner together the night before—maybe if we had been together in our favorite Chinese restaurant, soothed by the safe and familiar setting, sipping our lukewarm green tea, he would have told me about his plan.

I dialed 911 as if I were in a movie. The person I thought I knew better than anyone else in the world was dead by his own hand, and I had been unable to stop it. Complicit in his murder, I was equally drenched in his blood.

A month later, recalling that scene in the office filled me with such dread that I rushed off the bus twenty blocks before I got to the church where the support group was meeting. How could I talk about the grisly details of Harry's death to people I had never met? As it was, I was lying about the circumstances to all but my immediate family and a few close friends. I told everyone that Harry's sudden death was caused by a massive heart attack. Why did his colleagues, our neighbors, his patients have to know what really happened? I knew they would ask me why Harry, an accomplished physician and medical researcher in the prime of his career, had decided to end his life, and I had no answers for their need to understand. I did not have the stomach to face their real or imagined accusations, blaming me—or blaming him—for his death. I had entered into a surreal world where accepted forms of mourning did not apply.

As I walked to the church, I felt faint and nauseous. I pictured a room filled with crazy people, the kind you see nodding and weaving in the streets. I imagined a revival meeting, with people boasting about salvation and forcing me, somehow, to embrace it. I was already ten minutes late when I spotted the sign, A SAFE PLACE, on the basement door of the church. I was cemented to the sidewalk, unable to move, when a silver-haired woman in a sleek fur coat came up behind me. "Are you here for the meeting?" she asked gently. I nodded and she guided me in, as if I were a blind person. I assumed she was the group's leader but soon found out she was a survivor like myself: One year before, during a Friday night dinner, her husband left the table, went into their bedroom, and shot himself with a pistol he kept in his night table. After calling the police, she sat calmly over their half-eaten meal, unable to believe what had just occurred.

We entered a small room with people sipping coffee from paper cups and eating cookies held on napkins. I was convinced that I was at the wrong place; everyone looked so normal. So ordinary. Many of them had come directly from work or school, and briefcases and book bags leaned casually against the wall. People seemed to know one another, laughing as they exchanged pleasantries.

Laughing! Small talk! Such modest luxuries seemed forever out of my reach. I was consumed with Harry's death, exhausted from replaying the details of his last days and final minutes over and over in my mind. I had spent hours obsessively searching for overlooked clues that might explain his reasons for ending his life. I was plagued by questions that only he could answer. Why? Why? Why? buzzed inside my brain like a swarm of bees, threatening to destroy whatever sanity I had left.

Since Harry's suicide, I felt increasingly isolated from my friends and family. They had no idea what I was going through, all their well-intentioned advice and words of comfort seeming ignorant at best and tinged with cruelty at worst. Yet, here I was with others who had supposedly experienced the nightmare of suicide, and I still felt alone and unconnected. Trapped and claustrophobic, I started to leave without even removing my coat.

"Please stay here with us," the man who suddenly appeared at my side said in a French-tinged accent. I later found out he was Jean-Claude Deshauteurs, the facilitator of the group and a volunteer at Samaritans, the suicide prevention group that sponsored these free meetings twice each month. I felt raw and exposed, and I had the startled look of a newcomer to a strange world. "You're among friends," he said.

He gently steered me to the adjoining room, where folding metal chairs had been set up in a large circle. There were no windows in this bleak basement, and the cheerful posters on the walls only served to call attention to the starkness of the space. I still refused to take off my coat, even though I sat down in the chair he offered me next to his. Slowly, the circle began to fill with normal, everyday people—a typical New York crowd that blended ages, ethnic backgrounds, and economic classes.

I was in a daze as Jean-Claude welcomed us to the meeting. Tension now filled the air, choking out the seemingly casual mood of minutes before. We were getting down to business. Jean-Claude thanked us for coming and asked us to state our first name, our relationship to the person who had committed suicide, and how and when they had killed themselves. After the introductions, he explained, there would be an open discussion.

The woman to my right started sobbing; I was stunned. Had all the people in this room—these "normal" people—really been through a suicide? Did they all feel as guilty as I? Were their lives, too, shredded beyond recognition? The kindly woman who had led me into the meeting, the athletic young man in his college sweatshirt, the businessman whose booming laugh so inappropriately filled the room as he had passed around the plate of cookies? I willed myself to concentrate, an ability I was convinced I had lost forever with Harry's death.

Jean-Claude turned to the man sitting on his other side, motioning him to begin. "My name is Ray," he said. "My brother hung himself two years ago at Bear Mountain State Park. He was thirty-six, my younger brother."

"My name is Elizabeth. My father shot himself last year on Thanksgiving Day. It was two hours before we were going to

9

eat. My family had gathered together from all across the country in our childhood home in Iowa. We spent the holiday scrubbing his brains off the dining room wall."

Elizabeth began sobbing. A box of tissues was passed around the circle to her. Like the children's game Hot Potato, the tissues would end up on the lap of the person who was crying the hardest. "I'm sorry, this is my first meeting and I'm terrified," she apologized. "I didn't have the courage to come before now."

"I'm Ivan. My son jumped in front of the subway four months, two weeks, and three days ago. He had just entered his sophomore year of high school and was returning from class."

"My name is Cheryl. My mother took an overdose of pills on her seventy-fifth birthday. It was six weeks ago. She left a note saying that she didn't want to be a burden to her children in her old age. She had been dead two days before I found her."

It did not stop. There were aunts and boyfriends, wives and grandfathers, best friends and fathers.

"Hi, I'm Victoria. My husband was one of the most prominent heart surgeons in the country. Three years ago, he jumped from the window of our Park Avenue apartment. A policeman called me at our country home in Connecticut. 'I'm sorry to tell you,' he said, 'but your husband has taken his life.' 'Taken it where?' I demanded to know. 'No, you don't understand, ma'am. He took his life. You know, death.' I yelled at him, 'You sick son of a bitch,' and slammed down the phone. He called back immediately. If it wasn't so insane, it would have been funny."

"My name is Hal. I found my fourteen-year-old daughter in the bathtub with her wrists slit on July 8, 1989, six months ago. I was devastated at first but now I'm getting on with my life. I'm moving on and trying not to dwell on it."

"I'm Kevin. I was eleven when my father shot himself in our basement. It was the day before he was to retire as a New York City police detective. I found him when I came home from school. That was nine years ago—I'm now a junior at college—and all of a sudden I want to talk about it. You see, my father was my hero. He was always getting medals for bravery and I wanted to be just like him. But he left my mother and my six brothers and sisters alone to clean up after his shit. Now I think he's a fucking coward." An animal-like cry, combining fury and agony, erupted from deep in his chest. The tissues started making their way over to him, but he waved them away.

"Kevin, we'll come back to you when we're finished with the introductions," Jean-Claude spoke calmly.

"I am Bernice. I am here today because my therapist suggested that it might help. I came home from work last April and found my lover with a bag on his head and a bunch of pills by his side. He had lung cancer and was in a lot of pain. I am worried because I don't feel anything—sadness, anger, fear—nothing. I think that I will never feel anything again."

"My name is Joe. My father jumped off the roof of his apartment building two years ago last September. My mother had died the month before after suffering from a debilitating stroke for three years. They were married forty-six years, and my father had taken care of her day and night. After he killed himself, I tried going to a psychiatrist to figure it all out. He told me that my father was 'success-oriented.' I swear. He told me that my father had made up his mind to kill himself and he had accomplished his goal. Spare me, Doctor. If he's such a success, why is he six feet under?"

Laughter rippled through the room, relieving some of the pressure.

"I'd rather not say my name. My twin sister strangled herself five months ago. She tied her sheets to the bedpost and then crawled along the floor. I didn't even know you could kill yourself that way. She was in a psychiatric hospital upstate— under suicide watch, no less. I had her committed because she was repeatedly threatening to kill herself. I guess you can't save them if they won't let you."

"My name is Earl. My wife killed herself one year ago yesterday. She turned on the car in the garage and died from the carbon monoxide fumes. My two kids and I were asleep in the house, so I don't know what she was thinking. She once told me she wanted to be cremated, have her ashes thrown in our garden. Do you know there are bone fragments in that stuff? The wind kept blowing them back in my face."

"My name is Carla, and this is my first meeting. It's my husband's birthday today; he would have been forty-four. He killed himself four weeks ago. He was a doctor, so he injected himself intravenously with some heavy-duty anesthetic. Up until tonight, I didn't know there were so many other people who could understand what I was talking about." The box of tissues was on my lap before I realized that tears were streaming down my face. The crying in the room assured me that I was not alone.

I suddenly remembered that I was still wearing my coat and began struggling to remove it. Jean-Claude leaned over to help me.

"I'm glad you've decided to stay, Carla," he said.

Seeing Hal from that bus window brought back vivid recollections of this first meeting. I thought about the singular bond suicide survivors share with one another. Even though each of our situations is unique, we all experience similar stages in our grieving. When we meet someone else who has *been there*, it makes our personal chaos and isolated secrecy seem a little less frightening.

Suicide is different from other deaths. We who are left behind cannot direct our anger at the unfairness of a deadly disease or a random accident or a murderous stranger. Instead, we grieve for the very person who has taken our loved one's life. Before we can even begin to accept our loss, we must deal with the reasons for it—and the gradual recognition that we might never know what happened or why.

According to the book *Suicide and Its Aftermath: Understanding and Counseling the Survivors*, edited by Edward Dunne, John McIntosh, and Karen Dunne-Maxim, the attention of the mental health profession focuses on those who commit suicide and rarely addresses what happens to people who have survived the suicide of someone close to them. The authors cite studies showing that people who lose a loved one to suicide feel more guilt, more often search for an understanding of the death, and appear to experience less social support than those who lose a loved one to other causes.

In addition, the authors write, suicide survivors experience feelings of intentional rejection and deliberate abandonment, which separate them from others who are mourning the death of a loved one. They state: "This difference may explain why survivors of suicide who have attended grief groups for survivors of deaths by other causes report feeling different from other grievers and tend to drop out of these groups."

Suicide is the eighth leading cause of death in the United States and the third leading cause of death among young people ages fifteen to thirty-four. The American Association of Suicidology estimates that for each of the 32,000 Americans who kill themselves each year, there are six survivors. According to the association, there are approximately 4 million people in the United States who have lost a loved one to suicide, with the number increasing annually by almost 200,000 persons.

Yet, most of us who have experienced the suicide of a loved one feel separate and apart. At the time my husband killed himself, it seemed inconceivable that I would ever emerge from the isolation created by his death. Even in my self-exile, however, I knew that there must be others who understood what I was going through. I searched fruitlessly in the literature for books and articles containing stories similar to mine. Instead, I found medical texts analyzing why people kill themselves, manuals on suicide prevention, articles on the link between creativity and suicide, essays on the moral and philosophical implications of suicide, even guidebooks on how to kill yourself; those of us who were left behind seemed forgotten, overshadowed by the drama and mystery that suicide leaves as its legacy.

I am writing this book because I do not want our stories to go untold. The grieving process of suicide survivors is often shrouded by stigma and silenced by shame. By exchanging the unthinkable details about our mother's swallowing an overdose of pain medication, our son's shooting himself with a hunting rifle, our brother's jumping from an office window, our wife's poisoning herself with carbon monoxide fumes, we will come to realize that we are neither crazy nor alone.

Since my husband's death, I have spoken with more than one hundred women and men throughout the country who are struggling to find meaning from their loved one's suicide. They have revealed their most carefully guarded personal histories to me in the hope that their stories might help ease the pain of others in similar circumstances. I have changed their names and some of the details of their stories because I believe that privacy and secrecy are two separate entities: We can own and protect our privacy without being made to feel that we are hiding some dark, shameful secret. In addition, I have interviewed a number of mental health professionals and others who specialize in the field of suicide survivors.

It is my hope that by sharing our experiences, the loneliness of mourning our loved one's self-inflicted death will begin to diminish. As instant comrades-in-arms in a common struggle, we can identify with the stages and patterns of our similar journeys. We will see that, ever so slowly, the pain does ease. Gradually, there will be minutes, then hours, then longer chunks of time when the suicide is not the focus of our lives. Even though we have entered a looking-glass existence, where everything we once held dear has been transformed beyond recognition, we will come to believe that eventually we will emerge. And survive.

"I refuse to make two tragedies out of this," says Carol, a woman whose husband drowned himself when she was nine months pregnant. "As much as I want to die, I know I want to live. The choice is as simple as that."

I have worked hard to overcome the gripping shame that continues to cloud my acceptance of Harry's decision to die: Seven years after his suicide, the words "he killed himself" are still uncomfortable for me to say when I am asked about the cause of his death at the age of forty-three. Yet, as I start to talk about it more openly, what most surprises me is the reaction to my decision to tell the truth: "My sister killed herself in her freshman year of college," a neighbor confides. "My uncle drove his motorcycle into a tree," the dental assistant reveals. "My father shot himself," the woman sitting next to me on the flight to Miami whispers.

I hope this book will help penetrate the isolation that

surrounds the mourning process of those of us who have lost a loved one to suicide. As we begin to tell our stories, the stigma associated with the memories of our mothers and fathers, husbands and wives, sons and daughters, sisters and brothers, lovers and friends, relatives and coworkers, will be lifted. With the support of others who have been there, we will be able to let go of the silence and start to make sense of the chaos that suicide leaves behind.

Part Two

THE SUICIDE

The World Explodes

In the days following my husband's suicide, I remembered a documentary about cancer patients that I had seen several years before. A woman dying of leukemia spoke of her decision to wait twenty-four hours before telling her family and friends about her confirmed diagnosis.

"As soon as my doctor gave me the results of my blood test, I entered into another world," she explained. "I knew that I would think of myself differently once I revealed that I was dying. I also knew I would be treated differently. For as long as I could, I wanted to be like everyone else."

In my mourning, I, too, wanted to be like everyone else. I wanted my family and friends to comfort me, not to question me about why Harry had killed himself. I wanted to grieve my husband's absence, not analyze his reasons for dying. I wanted to celebrate his kindness and friendship throughout our twenty-one years of marriage, not to rage at him for abandoning me in the prime of our lives.

The suicide of a loved one irrevocably transforms us. Our world explodes, and we are never the same. Most of us adapt, eventually learning to navigate on ground we no longer trust to be steady. We gradually come to accept that our questions will not be answered. We try not to torture ourselves for having failed to predict the coming catastrophe and preventing our loved ones from taking their lives.

"My crystal ball was cloudy that day," says Eric, whose sister took an overdose of sleeping pills on her thirtieth birthday. "If I had known four years ago what I know now, maybe I could have stopped her suicide or at least postponed it. But I couldn't see the future. I can't keep blaming myself for her death if I am to begin to think about her life. And it is a life worth remembering."

I, too, wished I could have seen the future and stopped my husband from killing himself. After Harry's suicide, I repeatedly scrutinized the events leading up to it, turning every fact I could unearth on every side possible. I imbued myself with the most minute details of what I believed to be the chronological sequence of the last hours, minutes, and seconds of his life.

I continually fantasized different scenarios in order to create a different ending. I would say the right words, make the right gesture, enter the room at the right time. Then, as if in a movie, the frame would freeze and the action would stop. But no matter how many times I rewrote and rescripted, Harry always died. I would never know what he was thinking, how long he had planned for his death, why he had taken his life at this particular moment in time, and, most excruciating, what I might have done differently to save him. Gradually, I began to understand that in order to accept his death and commemorate his life, I would have to forgive both of us for what had taken place.

Harry had been very depressed since the deaths of both his parents in the preceding year. I remembered the terrible anguish I suffered from my own father's sudden death fourteen years earlier, and so I accepted Harry's explanation that his double loss accounted for his darkening moods and increasing agitation. Throughout our entire marriage, Harry had recurring bouts of what he called melancholia and I referred to as "black clouds" that always seemed to pass over after several days. He spoke freely and openly about his two suicide attempts at the age of seventeen, attributing them to a troubled teenager's desire to get attention from parents whom he considered remote and judgmental.

Harry and I married in college. Although he was born and raised in Colombia, South America, his parents were refugees from the Holocaust who fled Vienna in 1938. He was deeply affected by the fact that his intellectual father, a prominent lawyer in Austria, was forced to support his family in his new country by becoming a zipper salesman. Harry claimed he would rather die than give up his dream of becoming a physician.

Ironically, Harry killed himself just as he was becoming extremely successful in his medical career: His private practice was booming; he had been recently appointed an assistant professor on the faculty of a prominent medical school; and he was beginning to achieve recognition as a pioneering researcher in the field of urology, having just published his fourteenth article in a leading medical journal.

Harry's dedication to his work seduced me from recognizing the truly despondent state of his mind. Even now, I still find it almost impossible to understand how he was able to treat patients two hours before executing his own death. Like most other survivors, the option of suicide seemed inconceivable to me at the time. Sure, Harry was depressed. Of course I could understand his sadness at his parents' deaths. Yes, I could see that he was becoming withdrawn from me and that our marriage was suffering. "I'll get over this," Harry promised me, and I allowed myself to believe him.

Like Eric's, my crystal ball is much clearer now. In razor-edged sharpness, I can reconstruct the various signs of Harry's foreplanned death. I recall his reaction when a medical colleague killed himself on a steamy August night, less than six months before Harry's own suicide. I had received a telephone call from a mutual friend explaining how Chris had left his hospital in a small Texas town after completing evening rounds, had driven to a nearby lake, and shot himself in the head with a gun he kept in the trunk of his car.

I decided not to tell Harry until he came home from his own hospital rounds because I did not want to give him such devastating news on the telephone. But I was unprepared for his reaction. "He really showed those sons of bitches," he replied, without even knowing the context of Chris's suicide. There was an almost-triumphant smile on Harry's face, which so frightened me that I was unable to ask him what he meant. As I map out the signs that led to Harry's own suicide, I see that his eerie response that evening reflected a deep inner turmoil that was too terrifying for me to acknowledge.

I also remember the sadness that never left him after his

mother suffered a stroke two years before she eventually died. His father had called from Colombia to say that although her condition was serious, the doctors assured him that she would not suffer any permanent impairment. Harry flew down immediately, taking with him medication that was difficult to obtain in Colombia and copies of articles for the doctors describing the most advanced treatments for stroke victims.

Harry returned the next week, a different man. "My mother is gone," he reported, in an undramatic, clinical tone. "She can speak, even remember, but her soul has been eradicated." Harry had gone to the hospital directly from the airport. His mother was lying in bed in elegant bedclothes, her hair coiffed, her nails manicured—as always, the dignified Viennese lady. When Harry went to kiss her, his father prompted her, "You know who this is, don't you?" She replied, "Of course, this is my son, Harry."

From the day he was born, Harry's mother called him by the nickname "Strupy." I never heard her refer to him in any other way, whether she was talking to him or talking about him. After her stroke, she never called him that again. Harry's diagnosis was irrevocable: "Even though my mother is able to give what she knows to be the correct answers, she has no memory of emotions," he told me. "I have lost her forever."

I pinpoint that conversation as the moment when the spirit started ebbing out of Harry. It was almost as if he had joined with his mother, responding and acting in a socially appropriate manner but without any sense of joy or hope. Our once complex and rich relationship—previously filled with discussions, disagreements, and eventual détentes—started straining as two longtime partners slowly became strangers, each of us struggling alone with our own private terrors.

Over the following two years, Harry flew back and forth to Colombia on a frequent basis, each trip sapping more of his diminishing reservoir of optimism. One weekend when he was down there, his mother died of a second, more powerful stroke. Harry returned with one of his "black clouds" over his head. This time, I knew it was neither temporary nor without risk. It darkened, it strengthened, and it spread. Five months after his mother's death, Harry's father called to say that his colon cancer, which had been in remission for ten years, had spread to his liver. Within the year, he, too, was dead.

Looking back, I know the exact moment when I lost Harry. He and his father had a turbulent relationship, suffused with explosive arguments, dramatic reconciliations, and long periods of silence. Yet, in his capacity as physician to his father, Harry could function without any internal conflict. He did not have to resolve his role as the loving son in order to provide his father with the best medical care and caring possible. Again, Harry flew back and forth to Colombia practically every other weekend. He was living on adrenaline and an almost desperate battle to defeat death.

He was in the middle of seeing patients when I got the call that his father had died. Harry had just returned from Colombia three days earlier, announcing in a flat voice that his father would not last the week. I walked over to his office, carrying the bad news with me like a ticking bomb. I sat with his secretary in the crowded waiting room. When Harry saw me, he waved me into his consultation area. Before I could open my mouth, he cut me off. "When did he die?" he asked.

"An hour ago." I went to hug him, to comfort him, but he pushed me away angrily.

"I still have patients to see, so you better go," he dismissed me.

That is when my husband slipped away from me. The cruelty in his voice and the coldness in his actions were like being punched in the stomach.

"I'll make the airline reservations." I got up from my chair in a daze.

"What makes you think I'm going to the funeral? I just saw him. You think I give a shit what the community down there thinks about my being there?"

Harry was in a rage. Even though he never attended temple, Harry had a healthy respect for the cultural aspects of the Jewish religion. As the oldest son of an observant father, he was defying the gods by refusing to attend the funeral. He knew it and he welcomed it.

We had the worst fight of our marriage that night. I could not believe he would not be saying the prayers at his father's gravesite the next day. He shouted that it was none of my business and that I better shut up because he was feeling violent. We screamed at each other until we finally fell asleep from pure exhaustion. Harry had scheduled early morning surgery at the hospital, and he left the house as if nothing were wrong.

Three months after his father's death, having carefully researched how best to carry out his own execution, Harry was dead by lethal injection. During this period, as Harry sank farther into a black hole of despair, we fought constantly. I finally made it a condition of our marriage that he seek professional help. After one session, Harry dismissed the first psychiatrist he saw—a widely respected expert on depression—as a pompous jerk. Next, he went for several visits to a social worker who specialized in crisis counseling. He then refused to continue treatment because the social worker was, as Harry put it, too enamored by the simplistic twelve-step recovery movement.

But then Harry offered me a deal, one that I accepted against my better judgment. After returning from a lovely walk in the park with our black Labrador, Cinco, Harry made a proposal. He asked me to look at our twenty-one-year marriage as a bank account with credits and debits. He said that the glorious times we'd had together over the years should be viewed as credits. Now, his increasingly bizarre behavior—caused, he theorized, by the temporary blow of his twin tragedies—should be considered as debits. He was withdrawing money from the bank, but his history should be sufficient to extend his account. In other words, stand by him a little longer.

Weeks after Harry's death, when I was finally able to clean out his office, I found pages and pages of computer printouts from the National Institutes of Health, cross-referenced under "Suicide" and "Drugs." He had started conducting the research around the same time he asked me to give him a chance and continue to trust him after two decades of marriage.

The conclusion of the article abstracts that Harry had circled was that Thiopental, used to execute prisoners in some states where capital punishment is legal, was the most effective drug available. Five months after Harry's suicide, Dr. Jack Kevorkian helped his first client, Janet Adkins, inject Thiopental into her veins, bringing about her death within minutes. Once, when I was reviewing with my lawyer the dismal financial situation left by Harry's suicide, I remarked to him that even though Dr. Kevorkian was getting rich and famous in the suicide business, at least he had the good sense to use Thiopental on others and not on himself. As it was, it took me almost a year before I was able to pay the medical supply company where Harry had charged his order for ten bottles of Thiopental: I finally bought a money order for $240, because I was physically unable to sign my name to a personal check.

Harry called me several hours before he killed himself, saying he would be working late in the office. He sounded somewhat sad, not wanting to get off the phone even as his secretary apologetically buzzed into our conversation to tell him that his patients were becoming restless.

Something about our conversation made me nervous. By the end of the day, my repeated calls were being picked up by his answering machine, so I decided to walk over to his office. It was then that I entered his examining room, suffused with the smell of death. The police were there within minutes after my call, young men visibly shocked that a physician had chosen to use his own medical skills to kill himself.

They led me into the lobby of the building, asking me to wait there for the detectives. Sometimes I picture myself being hysterical; other times I think I was calm. I do remember using the doorman's telephone to call my close friend Alex. He lived nearby and it seemed that as soon as I put down the receiver, he was magically sitting by my side on the brown leather couch in the suddenly very busy lobby.

The building was hopping. The police cars, ambulances, emergency service vehicles outside had attracted a circuslike crowd. The superintendent, who could never be found in the best of times, was talking nonstop to any police officer who would speak to him. Maintenance workers emerged from the basement to sweep the lobby. Residents of the building came down to walk their dogs, check their mail. The honest ones just stood in front of me and gawked.

"Your husband is dead," the detectives, two broad-shouldered men dressed in suits and ties, told me. Even though they were gentle, one of them even putting his arm around my shoulders, I screamed from my very depths: "He killed himself, right? He killed himself."

There is no dignity or privacy in suicide. The police, the super, the dog walkers, the gawkers all found out that my husband killed himself at the same exact time it was confirmed to me.

The detectives took notes as they questioned me. What was the financial state of Harry's medical practice? Had we been experiencing any marital problems? Did he have a drinking problem? When was the last time I had seen him alive? Was I a nurse? Did I have any experience with intravenous drugs?

Through my disassociated haze—nothing seemed quite real to me—I began to grasp that I was being treated as a suspect. "Do you actually think I killed my husband?" I remember asking them.

The detectives were kind, closing their notebooks before their next question might possibly send me over the edge. They told Alex he could take me home, I did not have to wait for the medical examiner to arrive. They gave me their cards, writing the telephone number of the medical examiner's office on the back and telling me to contact them at the precinct if I needed their assistance.

As we left the lobby, I saw the medical examiner getting out of his car. His black leather bag was similar to the one I had given Harry as a present when he graduated medical school. There was yellow police tape draped in front of the entrance to Harry's office. It was right out of a crime scene in the movies. It *was* a crime scene.

Bruce Danto writes in *Suicide and Its Aftermath: Understanding and Counseling the Survivors* that the standard practice of treating a suicide as a homicide until evidence proves to the contrary compounds the difficulties the survivor has dealing with the death. He explains that most people are unfamiliar with official police procedures, and the "suggestion that they may be a murder suspect is difficult to cope with under the circumstances and can result in increased despair and anger toward the police officer."

The fact that suicide is considered a criminal act comes as an abrupt shock to most survivors. Even as we are trying to absorb the unexpected and often violent deaths of our loved ones, we find ourselves dealing with the intricacies of a law enforcement system that is largely unfamiliar and somewhat threatening to us. If we are lucky, the police are sensitive; if we are confronted with hostile accusations, our self-ordained role as an accomplice to a murder is confirmed and validated.

I knew I had to make telephone calls. Harry's brother, from whom he was estranged after his refusal to attend his father's funeral. My mother. My sisters. His close friend in Bogotá. My best friend in Oregon.

Although chaos whirled around me, I was calm in the eye of the storm. It seemed as if the unfolding events were happening to some other person. I was quite organized: Harry was to be buried in my family cemetery in Massachusetts, as close to my father as possible. My sister was to get me the pertinent information—the name of the funeral home that had handled my father's burial, details about purchasing a cemetery plot, the arrangements I'd have to make for transporting the body out of state. I gave clear instructions: Anyone who asked must be told that Harry had died of a heart attack. There were to be no exceptions.

A representative from the funeral home called me back immediately. He assured me that he would coordinate all the details relating to Harry's burial. I was fully in control as I answered his questions. I gave him the relevant telephone numbers in New York. I told him I wanted a simple pine coffin, a traditional white shroud. I said that I needed a rabbi to conduct the prayers at the cemetery. I confirmed that I would be paying by check.

And then he asked if I would be buying a single plot or a

double. It was as if someone had taken a blowtorch and melted the frigid ice cabinet in which I had been encased.

"How dare you ask me that?" I howled from a primal spot deep within my chest. "I'm not dead, do you hear me? Why would I want to be buried with my husband? I'm still alive. I didn't die."

Of course, I now accept his question as standard in the funeral business. And maybe if my husband had really died of a heart attack, I might have considered his inquiry to be thoughtful. After all, Harry and I had been married for twenty-one years. Married couples buy double plots—even common tombstones—all the time, planning years ahead to be buried next to each other. But I heard only accusation, not comfort, in his tone, confirming my deepest fears that my failure to keep Harry alive had made me an accessory in his death.

That night, I refused to take tranquilizers to calm down or go to sleep. I had to remain alert, a soldier on the lookout for further sneak attacks. Only this time, I would not be caught off guard or unprepared.

During the months that preceded Harry's suicide, I had confided to very few people my fears about his increasingly irrational behavior. One of the people I did feel safe talking with was an old high school friend now living in Boston. Dana had recently gone through some very difficult times herself, and her empathetic advice had given me much needed strength to deal with events that seemed to be rapidly spiraling out of my control.

It must have been three in the morning when I called Dana with the news of Harry's suicide. She listened patiently, reassuring me again and again that his death was not my fault, that there was nothing I could have done to stop it. She then told me that one of her good friends had a brother who had recently killed himself.

"Let me have her call you," she suggested. It seemed pointless to me. My husband's body was still at the city morgue. I was telling the truth about Harry's suicide only to close friends and family. Why should I reveal what had happened to a perfect stranger? Besides, losing your brother was different from losing your husband.

"Trust me," Dana urged. "She has been where you are now."

Five minutes later, the phone rang. "Carla, this is Dana's friend, Nancy," she said in a voice that gave no indication that she had been sleeping. "Seven months ago, my kid brother shot himself in the chest. He was thirty-eight years old."

"Did you find him?"

"No, his wife did," Nancy answered matter-of-factly. "She said there was blood all over the house."

I wanted to know everything. It felt as if I were a reporter for the *National Enquirer*: The more sensational, more personal the details, the better.

For two hours, Nancy threw me a lifeline. She told me about the shock, the violence, the nightmares, the chaos her brother's death had left in its wake. She talked about her regret at not being able to say goodbye to him. Her conviction that his suicide was the ultimate "fuck you." Her sorrow for the desperation she knew he must have been feeling when he pulled the trigger. Her guilt for not having returned his morning phone call. Her anger at his leaving her alone with their shared childhood memories. She described how her moods fluctuated dramatically from moment to moment, constantly reconfiguring as if trapped in a twirling kaleidoscope.

Shafts of the rising sun were just beginning to fill my

apartment. Nancy then listened sympathetically to my obsessive recounting of the lurid chronology leading up to Harry's suicide. She understood perfectly about feeling guilty and ashamed. She appreciated my need to lie and cover up the truth. She empathized with my isolation, my feelings of madness.

I will never forget that talk with a stranger in the middle of the night. Our conversation gave me the courage to face the first task of the new morning: identifying the body. Identifying my husband. Identifying Harry.

Alex accompanied me to the medical examiner's office, in a nondescript building that housed the city morgue. If this were a real death, I thought, if this were a normal death, right now I would be sitting in temple, crying during Harry's funeral service. Instead, I was surrounded by dazed strangers sitting on plastic chairs, waiting for our names to be called out so we could confirm that it was indeed the body of our sister who had been murdered or our son who had been run over or our husband who had died by his own hand.

Alex and I were ushered into a windowless cubicle. The air felt heavy and stagnant. Color Polaroid mug shots of Harry lay on the desk. His face was smeared with blood and there were dark brown stains on his pink shirt. For the first time in my life, I fainted.

The staff, city workers who are routinely criticized by the public and the press for their callous indifference to their jobs, were compassionate and gracious. I was given a paper cup of orange juice. Alex was permitted to identify the photographs. A wet paper towel was placed on my forehead.

I felt as if I was having an out-of-body experience, and panic swept over me. I could not believe that any of this was actually happening. Alex led me out into the cold December morning.

"Maybe we should put off going to the police," he counseled. "Let me take you home."

But I wanted it all over with as soon as possible. I needed
clearance from the police to enter Harry's office, to return to
the scene of the crime. I needed to be able to sift for evidence,
to search for clues, to find some answers.

I had never been inside a police station before. There were
men being handcuffed and booked, women crying into pay
phones, officers drinking coffee from deli takeout containers.
The detectives invited us to sit in their office upstairs. We
waited there for several hours, until they officially ruled
Harry's death a suicide and closed the case. The medical examiner could now release his body to the funeral home. I
could pick up Harry's personal belongings—his wallet, his
wedding ring, his watch—at police headquarters. I could rip
the yellow police tape off the door to Harry's office. Clorox
was recommended for removing the blood from the floors and
walls. As their ringing beepers called the detectives away to
cases that had not yet been resolved, we exchanged final
handshakes. I appreciated the genuine concern I could see in
their eyes.

As I entered Harry's office, I was greeted by the red light
on the answering machine blinking frantically in the darkened
reception area. My thoughts started racing: Who would take
care of Harry's patients? I had to find another doctor to take
over the practice. Harry's secretary needed to be informed,
the hospital notified. The extent of what Harry had left me
with began seeping into my consciousness.

Furniture in the office had been knocked over, papers
were strewn about, the IV pole had fallen on top of the bloodied examining table. The claustrophobic atmosphere evoked
the medical examiner's office; again, I could not breathe.

I was not ready to face my husband's killing grounds. I fled home, searching for safety. People skimmed by me on the street, on their way to buy groceries or go to the bank or visit a friend. How were such trivial activities still possible? My husband had just committed suicide and my life would never be the same. I had passed over into another world.

3

The Initial Impact

"Many deaths leave survivors with unfinished business, but few may be said to create more of it than suicide."

—Bruce Conley,
Suicide and Its Aftermath: Understanding and Counseling the Survivors

Suicides are messy deaths; there is nothing neat about them. The lives of those of us who are left behind have been shattered into thousands of tiny fragments, and we do not know how to begin cleaning up the devastating damage. Our loved ones have departed *by their own will*; even though they knew that they were planning to leave us forever, they did not give us the opportunity to bid them Godspeed.

As we go about trying to pick up the pieces of our former

existence, we are fearful that we will be haunted by the ultimate absence of knowledge for the rest of our lives. We will
never know the reason why our mother hanged herself or our
brother walked into the sea or our child threw herself in front
of a train. Yet, even though we must live without closure concerning their deaths, always wondering about the whys and
imagining the what-ifs, we eventually begin to regain a sense
of control in our lives as we continue to search for some kind
of logic to our losses.

"I rearranged the paintings in my living room every night
for four months after my son shot himself," says Charlotte, a
teacher from Des Moines. "I would drag the ladder from the
garage into the house, take all the pictures off the wall, and
move them around for hours. In the early morning, I would
carry the ladder back to its place. But, no matter how I
changed the paintings, I could never get the room to look
right."

Coping with any death is traumatic; suicide compounds
the anguish because we are forced to deal with two traumatic
events at the same time. According to the American Psychiatric Association's *Diagnostic and Statistical Manual of Mental Disorders*, the level of stress resulting from the suicide of a loved one
is ranked as catastrophic—equivalent to that of a concentra-
tion camp experience.

"It is the difference between going to war and seeing your
first casualty," explains Steve, a New York television producer
whose brother drowned himself two weeks after graduating
from law school. "The worst part of suicide is the shock of it.
When my mother died from breast cancer, I had already gone
through much of the grieving process. I suffered terrible sadness and pain with her death, but it is not the same as the
turbulence and destruction I associate with my brother's sui-

cide. His decision to die eclipses the very fact that he is no longer alive."

The initial impact of discovery scars us forever. The image of my husband's beloved green scarf, bloodied by his self-inflicted brutality, has branded itself permanently on my memory. Yet, even though we are left reeling in disbelief, those of us who have experienced the unspeakable trauma of a loved one's suicide eventually find the resources to carry on. "You suddenly find yourself struggling to survive and discover you have strengths you never knew existed," says Sandy, a Detroit housewife whose daughter jumped in front of a train six months after the birth of her first child.

"I was thirteen when my mother hung herself," relates Laurie, a forty-six-year-old singer who now lives in Los Angeles. "Although her death is with me every second of my existence, I try not to talk about it too much. People have a weird reaction when I tell them. But I'm not a freak and neither was she.

"The memories of that day are very vivid. I was out of school on summer vacation. It was a Sunday morning. I was asleep but woke up when I heard my mother come into my bedroom. She took off her glasses, then got into bed with me. She began to hug me and kiss me. But somehow her demeanor was different. Normally, she was a real talker, always telling me how much she loved me, how I was the greatest daughter in the world. But that morning she was totally quiet. She just kept touching me without saying a word.

"The truth was that she was staring straight through me. Her eyes, which were usually hazel-green, were bright green. It was the strangest sensation. We snuggled for what seemed like an hour to me and I loved every minute of it. I must have fallen back to sleep. When I woke up, I saw that she was gone but had left her glasses on the bureau. I thought that was very odd because she was blind as a bat and never went anywhere without them.

"I started walking around the house yelling, 'Mommy, here are your glasses.' My father was in the living room reading the newspaper. I asked him if he had seen her and he said no. I opened the doors to all the rooms in the house but I couldn't find her. This terrible sense of urgency swept over me and I knew something was wrong. I went outside to a neighbor's house but she said she hadn't seen my mother. All this time, I remember my father reading the paper, not saying a word.

"I came back into the house and went methodically, room by room, screaming, 'Mommy, Mommy.' I opened the door to the bathroom again but this time I went inside. She was hanging in the stall shower, my jump rope tied around her neck. Her head was cocked to the side, her tongue was hanging out of her mouth, and her eyes were wide open. I didn't know if she were dead or not.

"I started screaming, like some kind of animal sound. My father came running into the bathroom and I remember that I was scared he would have a heart attack when he saw her. My baby brother was toddling around, crying and scared.

"My father told me to get my older brother, who was still sleeping in his bedroom. He was sixteen. I ran into his room, punching him hard to wake him up. He raced to the bathroom, took one look at my mother, and ran to the kitchen to get a knife to cut her down. We carried her to her bed. My brother started blowing into her mouth to give her air because we thought she might still be alive. I guess my father called the police and they came right away.

"My father sent me upstairs to my room with my little brother. I forced myself to calm down and then went outside.

There were all these ambulances and police cars and people who were just standing around looking, like a carnival. I pretended to be a casual observer and went up to one of the policemen on the street. I asked him: 'Officer, what happened to the lady in there?' He answered, 'She passed away.' I began screaming at the top of my lungs, 'She was my mother. She was my mother.' All the neighbors just looked at me. Finally, some woman came out of the crowd and put her arm around me. She led me back inside the house. No one else moved; they just watched me.

"The police took my mother away. My father, brother, and I just sat together in the dining room and cried and cried. My little brother was also there crying, only he didn't know why. I felt like I wasn't really there with them. That I had died with my mother and I was just watching someone cry who used to be me. I left the house to take a walk. It was a beautiful day. I stopped by all the neighbors to tell them what happened, even though I'm sure everyone knew by then. I would repeat the details of the story, then keep on walking. We moved out of our house that night and I never slept there again.

"My family doesn't discuss my mother's suicide. Once it was over, it was never talked about again. But for awhile, I was obsessed about describing what happened to everyone I met. Then, as I got older, I stopped telling people. I believe that I have shelves in my life where my memories are stored. When I decide, I can take them down, dust them off, and then put them back. My mother's death is on one of those shelves. I now focus on the fact that she chose me to spend her last hour with, to tell me how much she loved me before she died. This gives me great comfort.

"My mother had a beautiful voice and I wanted to succeed

as a singer as a tribute to her. As a child, I held on to the idea that when I sang she would be listening to me in heaven, feeling very proud. I know that when I sing, part of her is within me. I am singing for both of us."

Laurie sobbed in anguish as she recalled the painful memories of her mother's death. Yet, like Nancy, who had reached out to me in the middle of the first terror-filled night following my husband's suicide, Laurie shared her story so that others who are suffering from similar experiences will realize they are not alone.

"I recently became friendly with an eighty-two-year-old woman whose father killed himself when she was seven," she says. "She tells me that his suicide seems as if it happened yesterday, that time has passed in the blink of an eye. I completely identify with her and feel very close to her. We are like members of a secret society. Maybe if survivors are more open about what happened to us, we can chip away at the wall of silence that surrounds suicide. Then, we can begin talking about our loved ones with pride, not shame."

The immediate response to suicide is total disbelief: The act itself is so incomprehensible that we enter into a state where we feel unreal and disconnected. "When I heard that my roommate from college had jumped out of his office window, it was as if I had been instantly thrust under water," describes Jay, a real estate broker from Tucson. "At the time I got the call, I was meeting with a client. After I got off the phone, I could see his mouth opening and closing but I couldn't understand what he was saying. I had separated from my surroundings and was suspended in air."

Even if there is a history of mental illness and past suicide attempts, we can never be prepared for the devastating shock of sudden self-death. Sarah is a graphic artist currently living in Philadelphia. Her younger sister, Melissa, suffered from anorexia and had been in and out of hospitals since her early teens. Although her sister had tried unsuccessfully to kill herself several times before, Sarah did not believe her mother when she called to say that Melissa had been found dead in her apartment with her wrists slit. She was twenty-six years old.

"My mother told me that Melissa was dead and I responded, 'Our Melissa?'" Sarah recounts. "I had been waiting for this call all my life but when it finally came, it didn't seem real. I went to work, spoke to my boyfriend, met a friend for lunch, but I never said a word all day about Melissa's suicide. Then, I went to my regularly scheduled therapist's appointment. I waited fifteen minutes into the session to tell her about my sister. I knew that the minute I gave it words, I could no longer deny what had happened. Melissa's suicide would now always be a part of my life."

Some of us walk in to discover our loved ones dead by their own hands; others are jolted with the news by a ringing telephone that instantaneously severs our lives into a "before" and an "after." For a number of survivors, the suicide takes place in front of their eyes. As if in slow motion, they watch the act unfold, powerless to reverse the death and destruction it leaves behind.

"My husband shot himself in our bed right after we made love," Gina, a twenty-nine-year-old nurse from Atlanta says unemotionally, the image too overwhelming to absorb even after ten years. "Scotty was a police officer and had just come home from the night shift. His uniform was draped on the chair next to the bed, so he was able to reach for his service revolver without getting up. It was like a dream. I watched him take his gun and point it to his head. He mouthed the words 'I'm sorry,' and then pulled the trigger. There was this explosion and I was instantly drenched with his blood and brains. It was warm all over me. The blood had a coppery odor, like a new penny, and it blended in with the sulfury scent of gunpowder. I can still smell it.

"I started screaming hysterically. I then ran out of the house, totally naked. One of the neighbors must have phoned 911 and the police came right away. They were very nice to me. One of them helped me into the shower so I could wash Scotty off me. He then helped me get dressed. The police were devastated that one of their own had taken his life. They called his parents, who lived nearby. When they arrived, they started screaming at me: 'Why didn't you tell us Scotty was depressed? Why didn't you call us?' Scotty and I had been married for less than a year. I was nineteen years old and didn't know any better. I had been very happy so I just assumed he was too.

"We were living in San Antonio and Scotty's suicide was in all the papers. One of the reporters found out from someone—I'll never know who—that I'd recently had an abortion. She wrote in her article that Scotty might have been depressed about that. That was almost as devastating as his death. I was having a difficult pregnancy and the doctors had advised me that my health was in danger. Scotty and I had agonized over the decision to end the pregnancy. It was he who urged me to do it, saying we could always try again soon. All of a sudden, it seemed as if everybody was blaming me for his death and I felt totally exposed.

"His funeral was very low-key. No one wanted to talk about how he died. To this day, his mother does not acknowledge that his death was suicide; she believes that somehow the gun went off accidentally. Even though his fellow officers came to Scotty's wake and funeral, none of them wanted to mention the word *suicide*. I thought I was crazy, like I was the only one who would say what was going on. Then I would think, maybe it is me who is nuts and Scotty really didn't mean to kill himself. But of course he did.

"I moved to Atlanta six months later and put myself through nursing school. Five years ago, I married a medical technician whom I had met at the hospital where we both work. We have a three-year-old daughter and our son is eight months old. I have never told anyone about Scotty's suicide—not even my husband. I'm afraid that if I say anything, his death will be thrown back in my face, as if it were my fault. One night, my husband and I were fighting about something. I get very quiet and distant when I get mad. My husband yelled at me, 'Your problem is that you don't know anything about suffering.' I thought, If you only knew, but I kept my mouth shut.

"I keep thinking about Scotty's death. I'm like a kid in front of the television set, replaying the Barney video over and over again. Only, with me, it's Scotty shooting himself all over me in our bed. Have you ever lost a filling in your tooth? You keep putting your tongue there to touch the empty space. That's what I feel like. I obsess about the what-ifs. What if I had stopped him from reaching for his gun? What if I had sensed that something was bothering him? What if I had decided to go through with the pregnancy? What if I had been more loving?

"I'll never know why Scotty did it. We didn't argue that night. Yet, he must have been angry about something, and I was the one who got the brunt of his anger. I feel that Scotty robbed me of the chance to be like everyone else, with a white picket fence and a 'normal' existence. I know that on the surface my life looks like that to others, but it feels like a big lie.

"Right after I moved to Atlanta, I started suffering severe panic attacks. I went to a therapist for two years but never told him about Scotty's suicide. You are the first person I have discussed this with. You interviewed a friend of mine whose brother killed himself. She's very open about his suicide but I have never told her about Scotty. She mentioned your name and I contacted you because I wanted my story to help others, if possible. I want people to know that you can go on, even though you're no longer whole."

Like Gina, suicide survivors are left to put their lives back together, even as we are haunted by our feelings of blame and self-doubt. Yet, before we can start to grieve for our loved ones, we must first get through the initial impact of their suicide. For months, the details of how Harry had died obscured the fact that I had lost my husband of twenty-one years. Gradually, I began to understand that his choice to end his life was separate from my feelings of loss at his absence. The unfinished business created by suicide overshadows the mourning process; we can begin to heal only if we are able to mourn.

"It feels as if it's been five hours, not five years since my son killed himself," explains Ted, a forty-nine-year-old architectural draftsman from a suburb of Seattle. "Jason drove his motorcycle off the road after having an argument with his girlfriend. He had just turned seventeen. He left us a note on the dining room table saying: 'I wish I had something to live for.' I used to talk about his suicide all the time, but I don't think people want to keep hearing about it. It's like they are saying, Why are you still reliving what happened after all this time? Get a life, already. But it feels as if I'm speaking about something different now. For the first two years, I was explaining what it was like to lose a son to suicide. Now, I'm describing what it's like to no longer have a son.

"Thoughts of Jason flood me. I can get transported back to places I've been with him just by hearing a certain sound. I try not to fight those feelings. Before Jason's death, I always accepted that life has its ups and downs and you just have to deal with them as best you can. But Jason's loss had an effect on me that I can't truly understand.

"My father died last year after being very sick from stomach cancer. His slow demise, no matter how painful, was part of nature. Jason's death was out of sequence. I remember his youth and vitality and spirit. A young person should not be thinking about death.

"Jason was doing very well in school. He was in his senior year and was planning to join the army after graduation. I always trusted that he knew the right thing to do. The other day I was in the gym and I saw a young man playing pool. When he finished, he put the cue back on the rack. He then turned off the light in the room. I noticed how he did all the right things, like Jason would have done. Yet, Jason did something so wrong when he killed himself.

"In a way, I feel deceived. Jason should have been able to share what he was feeling with me. I thought we were fairly close for a father and son. We both loved sports and would go to a couple of games together each year. I feel that he should have wanted to let me in on something that would have such a huge impact on my life. He knew how much I cared for him and yet he treated me like a stranger. He could have told me that he was hurting or in pain but he never let me know what he was planning.

"When I left for work the day Jason killed himself, my last words to him were, 'Is anything bothering you?' I knew he was having problems with his girlfriend; he had been moping around the house for a couple of days. He answered no, like kids do. I didn't want to push him because I wanted to give him some space. I thought he would just get over it like he usually did. By the end of the day, he was dead.

"My wife called me at work to tell me about the motorcycle accident. When I got home, there were all these police in my house. My wife was crying and showed me the note. I felt as if I had lost my mind, like I was on drugs and hallucinating. I went outside and began walking back and forth across the driveway. It seemed like an eternity. I was losing touch with reality. I was trapped. I thought, How can I live without him? It can't be. Where was Jason? Then it hit me that this was how it was going to be for the rest of my life.

"I got very angry at the police. I heard one of them talking about shift changes and I started screaming at him. I couldn't believe that in the middle of this horrible tragedy they could be talking about such mundane things as what time they should be getting off duty.

"The pain is something you have to experience. There is such a lack of control and there's nothing you can do about it. There is no answer. Crazy things happen in our world, but you can't dwell on why they're happening to you. It's just romanticizing your situation. With hope, you come to terms with it.

"I joined a local suicide survivor support group, which turned out to be my savior. Even though my wife has been in bad shape since Jason died, she didn't want to come to the meetings. If I didn't have the groups, my sense of isolation would have destroyed me. I saw that I was not alone in what I was experiencing. You have to try to reach out to people who have had a common experience and draw from it. It will help.

"Lately, the horror of the suicide has been replaced by good memories of Jason. I had been walling them off because I was scared that I wouldn't be able to handle them. I know I will never be the same person again but I also know I have to move on. Although I feel guilty that I'm alive while my son is dead, he will be in my heart forever. I have to let go of his suicide in order to reclaim his life."

Guilt suffuses every aspect of a survivor's healing process. Yet, in order to move on, we must begin to separate our loved ones from their suicides. Seven years later, I am finally beginning to define my husband's life by how he lived it—not by how he left it. It is not an easy journey.

I was recently invited to a neighbor's wedding. I attended reluctantly, afraid that I would be overwhelmed with reflections on my own marriage and regrets for what might have been. Yet, despite my fears, I found myself enjoying the evening. A wonderful swing band filled the hall with joyous music. I danced unencumbered, my body moving freely to the exuberant sounds. Suddenly, I realized that I still possessed a capacity for experiencing happiness; it had not died with Harry. It was like discovering an old friend I thought had been lost to me forever.

At the end of the set, the band leader made an announcement. The piece we had been dancing to had been written by him in honor of his father. As I applauded him along with the other guests, I saw it was Jack who was addressing the admiring crowd. Years before, we had occasionally attended the same survivor support meetings. A talented composer whose father had shot himself after losing money in the stock market, Jack had been terrified that he would never be able to create again after his father's suicide.

I caught his eye. His face lit up with a warm smile of recognition, a tribute to our individual endurance over these past years. Although we shared a secret pain that set us apart from the others, we both were aware that here he was, playing his life-affirming music, and here I was, dancing to it with pleasure.

The Final
Farewell

"Is suicide grief the worst, as is often suggested in the
literature?"

—John McIntosh,
Suicide and Its Aftermath: Understanding and Counseling the Survivors

The morning of Harry's funeral, four days after he killed himself, was so bitter cold that the grave diggers had trouble breaking open the frozen ground to lower his plain pine coffin. There were only six of us at the traditional Jewish ceremony held at the small cemetery in Massachusetts where my father, grandparents, and other members of my extended family were buried. The mood was tense and uneasy; Harry's was an angry death and our mourning reflected the absence of peace that surrounded it. Oblivious to the solemnity of the occasion, my dog, Cinco, raced excitedly from grave to grave, frolicking happily in the mounds of snow left by the past week's storm.

I had deliberately kept the funeral small. I could not face playing the role of grieving widow in front of a crowd of friends and relatives who might suspect that I was lying about the real cause of Harry's death. Some close family members who did know the truth about his suicide, however, chose not to attend the services for reasons they never explained to me. I interpreted their absence as a judgment against me: I was guilty, in their minds, for allowing my husband to die.

As the rabbi intoned the Jewish prayer for the dead over Harry's grave, I felt no sense of solace. I wrapped my wool coat tighter around my shaking body to protect myself not only from the frigid winds of the New England winter but also from the gusts of rage inside me. Harry had chosen to leave me without even saying goodbye, slamming the door in my face as he departed. I felt alone and abandoned.

Traditional funeral customs and rituals help mourners to restore a much needed sense of order to their disrupted lives. Yet, in death by suicide, even the observance of this universal passage is suffused with complications and uncertainty. Although many religious leaders now regard people who kill themselves as having suffered from a mental illness and not having committed a mortal sin, the act of suicide is still universally condemned by most major religions. As a result, the familiar anchors to which we normally cling for consolation and support during our grieving period are often not accessible to suicide survivors.

According to the book *The Jewish Way in Death and Mourning*, the "horror" of suicide is primarily moral—the betrayal of family and friends—not theological—the betrayal of God.

The book advises that "respect for the bereaved family must be scrupulously considered, as they are the sufferers and not the perpetrators of the act." Although there is no specific law against suicide in either the Bible or the Talmud, the book explains that if a death is judged self-inflicted, burial should be at least six feet from the surrounding graves, in a special section for suicides, or near the fence or border of the cemetery. No eulogy should be made for the suicide, "despite any good qualities he may have demonstrated in his life." Even so, the book states that because of the difficulty in determining a true suicide, "the rabbis have sought to deal leniently in their treatment of suicide."

The Christian view of suicide as sinful and forbidden evolved in the second half of the first millennium A.D., according to Charles Rubey and David Clark in *Suicide and Its Aftermath: Understanding and Counseling the Survivors*. They explain that the rites of burial were commonly refused to people who killed themselves, and this view had a direct impact on civil law in the West for centuries to follow. In many civil codes, suicide continued to be defined as a criminal act, with the heirs of suicide held responsible for the crime and deprived of their inheritances.

Over the last two decades, the legal, medical, and moral response to suicide has become more sympathetic, the authors relate. In addition, the religious perspective on suicide has evolved over the years to the point where suicide is no longer automatically considered a sin. Rubey and Clark theorize it is unlikely that God judges suicides as either moral or immoral, because a person who takes his or her life is experiencing the kind of pain that is the hallmark of illness or desperation. "God's judgment is likely to be based on a lifetime ledger of moral and immoral actions, not simply on the suicidal act that precipitated death," they write.

In the past, the rite of burial was offered strictly out of consideration for the deceased, the authors explain. In modern times, however, there has been an increasing recognition that religious ritual is also a significant source of comfort and closure for the survivors. Rubey and Clark believe that while the suicide should not be the focal point of the clergy's remarks at the funeral or the burial, neither should it be ignored.

Keith, a young playwright from New York City, found great comfort in his family's determination to be honest about his sister's suicide. "The minister, who knew our family, spoke about her valiant fight against depression," he says. "His eulogy referred to my sister's suicide in the context of an illness, not as a depraved act. Instead of being ashamed of how she died, I was proud about how she had lived."

The decision to allow traditional funeral services and burial procedures to be held for a person who has committed suicide is often left to the individual minister, rabbi, or priest. As a result, the course of a suicide survivor's mourning process can be profoundly affected by the degree of compassion and understanding extended by members of the clergy.

"I was brought up as a religious Jew and I was very ashamed that my wife had taken her life," says David, a government official from Washington, DC, who is in his late fifties. "As I understood it, suicide was considered murder and you couldn't be buried in the cemetery. The first rabbi I asked to officiate at the funeral barraged me with intimate questions about the details of my wife's suicide. His probing made me feel very uncomfortable and defensive.

"I then went to another rabbi, who was much more sympathetic. He helped me to understand that my wife was suffering from a mental illness, and that the Jewish religion is flexible enough to change its interpretations as more information about suicide becomes available. He reassured me that my wife could be buried in the Jewish cemetery with all the rituals. This rabbi was more concerned about how my children and I were dealing with our terrible loss than with the reasons why my wife had killed herself. He bestowed dignity not only to myself but also to my wife's memory."

Funerals are never easy; yet, with suicide, every decision takes on an added significance and importance. Details involving the type of ceremony, burial, eulogy, tombstone, and so on are influenced not only by how we judge our loved one's life but also by how comfortable we are with his or her death.

"My husband's family was ashamed of his suicide and did not want a funeral," says Kate, a thirty-six-year-old housewife from Memphis, who was left with three young children. "They said it wouldn't be helpful to anyone and we should hold a memorial service for him in six months when everything was 'cleaned up.' I had to fight them on it but I won. There were almost one hundred people in the church. I wrote a eulogy saying that my husband had been in a lot of pain and should be forgiven for killing himself. I also insisted on bringing my children to the services. I don't regret my decision for one minute."

Some survivors decide to hold a large funeral, even as they hide the truth about their loved one's suicide from relatives and friends. "My father was a well-respected businessman in town and my family didn't want the community to think less of him for taking his life," explains Juan, a college student from Houston. "We told everyone that he had died from a heart attack. Four hundred people came to his funeral; they practically didn't fit in the church. The minister talked about my father's 'love of life' in his eulogy. Two days later, the local newspaper reported that my father had died from carbon monoxide poisoning caused by automobile exhaust. When I saw the article, I felt doubly disgraced: First, for lying to people who cared for my father, and second, for being ashamed that he had killed himself."

There is a distinct sense of discomfort among the mourners at a funeral connected to suicide. "My next-door neighbor died during childbirth," relates Peggy, a twenty-six-year-old secretary from Long Island. "Her husband was distraught and didn't show up at her funeral. They broke into his house and found him hanging from the ceiling fan in the kitchen. Nobody wanted to talk about it. His funeral was so different from hers. Both were tragic in their own way, but no one spoke about how he had died. It was all so hush-hush."

Suicide not only opens up old wounds for family members but also creates new ones. "My son's funeral was filled with accusations and anger," describes Gloria, a retired day care worker from Chicago. "After my son married and had a child, he became estranged from me. He and I had an argument last Christmas and we stopped talking. Three months ago, my daughter-in-law called me at two in the morning to say that she had found him dead on the bathroom floor, a needle filled with heroin still attached to his arm. He had left a note, which she then proceeded to read to me. It said, 'May God forgive me for what I am going to do.' I thought she was playing a cruel joke on me. I just said okay and made myself go back to sleep. When I woke up, I knew it was true.

"I hated the funeral. I wasn't consulted on anything, as if his death were somehow my fault. I can't believe that my son died angry with me, yet I blame my daughter-in-law in part for his suicide. She should have seen it coming and tried to stop it. I guess I'll never find out what was going through his mind when he killed himself. All I know is that I feel dead, as if I'll never laugh or be carefree ever again in my life."

Kelly is a thirty-four-year-old social worker from Baltimore whose twin brother shot himself ten months ago after being laid off from his job. "The whole funeral was totally chaotic and unreal," she says. "I really didn't want to go. I flew down to his home in Little Rock in a state of shock. On the plane, I told the man sitting next to me that my brother had just killed himself. He was extremely sympathetic, explaining that his brother had also killed himself in Idaho more than thirty years ago. He was an older man and I imagined that his brother must have been Ernest Hemingway.

"My brother's wife wanted an open casket. Somehow they were able to put him back together but he looked so strange, almost as if he was pissed off about something. My mother was a wreck—sobbing, angry, and hurt. My father was very angry and two of my sisters refused to attend.

"I got the feeling from my sister-in-law's mother that she blamed my family for causing her daughter all this grief. After the services, she came up to me and said that it had cost her daughter four thousand dollars to clean up my brother's blood from the carpets and wallpaper in the house. She told me that her daughter didn't have that kind of money and I knew she wanted my family to offer to pay something. I just walked away from her. My brother and I were like one person, yet I felt very unemotional and detached during his funeral. Being there was the hardest thing I ever had to do in my life."

The decision to keep the casket open or closed is especially difficult for suicide survivors. "Even though my husband was physically wrecked, I was determined not to hide him in a closed coffin," declares Marie, a fifty-three-year-old widow of a prominent California politician who killed himself six years ago. "Tony shot himself in the head, so his injuries were extensive. I fainted at the medical examiner's office when I had to identify his body. The left side of his face was missing and his brains were falling out of a hole onto his shoulder. He was totally covered with blood. His right eye was wide open, as if in horror.

"Even so, I became obsessed with fixing Tony up so that his coffin could be open at the funeral. I paid a lot of money to embalm him and re-create his face. They cleaned off the blood, put his brains back in his head, and put wax on the entire left side of his head. Before the viewing, I would sit alone next to Tony's open coffin and read him his favorite passages from Shakespeare. I couldn't stop touching him. Finally, the funeral director told me not to hug his head so hard because the wax would probably come off under such pressure.

"By the last day of the viewing, his body began to smell like rotten meat. His was not a natural death; there was so much broken and destroyed about him. I was devastated when the funeral director told me that it was impossible to keep the casket open any longer.

"His funeral was huge. People came from all over, including the press. But all I kept on thinking was that everybody must be whispering that his coffin was closed because his body must be in such shambles. I was sure people were gossiping about what I might have done to make him want to kill himself. In order to get through the services, I encapsulated myself in a ball of light. I kept on repeating to myself over and over, 'The Lord is my shepherd,' and 'Forgive them, they know not what they say.' On the receiving line, I was like a robot. I just stood there, shaking people's hands and thanking them for coming. I felt insane, as if I were hanging on for dear life."

Like Marie and Kelly, whose twin brother shot himself, many suicide survivors comment on the fact that the bodies of their loved ones appear troubled, even angry in death. "I refused to believe it was my daughter at the funeral parlor," says

Shirley, a forty-seven-year-old bus driver from Buffalo. "She was such a lively young woman, only twenty-one years old, and this thing just lying there was not my daughter. Her skin was red from being refrigerated. She looked upset; her hands were almost in fists. I tried to smooth them down flat and fix her mouth in a smile. I kissed her and told her that she shouldn't have killed herself. But all the time I was talking to her, I really didn't believe it was my daughter.

"I wanted an open coffin and it was important that I pick out a special outfit for her to be buried in. I chose a suit we had just bought together two weeks before she killed herself. She had loved it. I also gave her my pearl earrings and pearl necklace.

"My daughter took an overdose of sleeping pills two years ago and part of me is still in denial about her being dead. I tell you, if my daughter walked through the door right now, I would believe it. It feels as if she left on a trip and will be back any minute."

Some suicide survivors are more comfortable with cremating their loved ones because cremation eliminates the need for a formal funeral, burial, and tombstone. Others choose cremation out of respect for their loved one's beliefs. Earl, a New York City police officer who is in his early forties, would have preferred to bury his wife with a traditional church ceremony but felt obligated to honor her last wishes.

"The day before my wife turned on the car engine in the garage and died from carbon monoxide fumes, she was working in our garden," he recalls. "I came home from work early and she was really glad to see me. She had been depressed recently but that afternoon she seemed happy. She looked young again, like when I met her in high school. As I started going into the house, she said to me, 'When I die, I would like to be cremated and have my ashes scattered in this garden.' I laughed her off, kidding that with my bad heart and big gut I would be dead long before she ever goes. She laughed along with me, but four days later I was spreading her ashes on the flowers. I miss not being able to go see her at the cemetery. Sometimes I walk around the garden but it doesn't feel the same."

Cemeteries, however, can also be unsettling for survivors, as Roger, a twenty-four-year-old video store manager from Denver, discovered when he visited his mother's grave last year, the first time since her funeral nineteen years earlier.

"For some reason, I was always afraid to go to the cemetery," he says. "Although my father told me the truth about my mother's suicide from the beginning, he would never go into detail about it with me. When I was growing up, I also spent a great deal of time with my mother's parents. They, too, never spoke about her or even had any of her photographs around the house. I had a very lonely childhood and was depressed all the time. Right before I was supposed to graduate from college, I swallowed a bottle of my father's heart medication. He found me unconscious when he came home from work and rushed me to the hospital. After they pumped my stomach, I was admitted to the psychiatric unit for thirty days. It was there that I began to realize the tremendous impact my mother's suicide had had on my life.

"It was my psychiatrist's suggestion to visit her grave. What really blew me away when I went there was that the only thing written on her tombstone was her name, date of birth, and date of death. All the other monuments had these elaborate inscriptions. It was like they just wanted to throw her in the ground and get rid of her. When I saw how lonely her grave looked, I started crying. It hurt me so much to think of her all alone there. I'm now considering asking my father and grandparents to put up a new tombstone or add something to the one already there. Part of me is afraid that they'll think I'm crazy for wanting to do it; that they'll tell me to just let it be. But I can't let her rest like that—so discarded and forgotten."

Alice, an elderly widow from a small town in Minnesota, removed the epitaph on her brother's tombstone when her children were little because she was afraid they would find out not only about his suicide but about her mother's suicide as well.

"Maybe if my children and grandchildren don't know what happened, it won't happen to them," she states. "I was seven and my brother was six when my mother took her life. It was seventy-two years ago and I can remember the scene as vividly as if it happened yesterday. My father was calling for her, 'Sweetheart, where are you?' Then, my brother and I were standing at the window, watching the police carrying her off. She had shot herself in the backyard. I can still picture the striped blue pajamas she was wearing.

"We didn't talk about it—it was too shameful. I thought she was crazy and that I would eventually go crazy too. My mother was pretty and smart. When people said I was like her when I was growing up, I didn't want to hear it. I was scared to be like her.

"Thirteen years after my mother's suicide, my baby brother killed himself. I was in the kitchen making fudge and a bullet came up through the kitchen floor. I ran downstairs to the basement. He had shot himself, like my mother, but he wasn't quite dead. On the way to the hospital, he pleaded with me to let him die, and he did die during surgery. My father was very angry at me for not saving my brother. He said I could have saved him if I had put a rag in his wounds. But I don't know if that's true.

"My brother left a note on his desk saying, 'Please forgive

me. There is no scandal—I just want to go on to better things.'
He was majoring in philosophy at college and also left one of
his philosophy books open to a page with the underlined
passage: 'A brave man is he who denies the will to live.' My
father put that quote on my brother's tombstone. When my
children were little, I hired a workman to scrape it off. I was
afraid they would ask me questions about what the words
meant.

"I don't talk about the deaths of my mother and brother
very much because of the terrible shame I feel. Sometimes, I
find myself crying, wondering why they took their lives. I
can't remember my brother ever being depressed. The afternoon he killed himself we were dancing in the snow in the
front yard. Then I went to make fudge and he went to study
his philosophy. I still don't understand what happened."

In burying our loved ones, we look for some kind of closure to their deaths. Randy is a veterinarian from San Diego
whose close friend hanged himself two years ago. He told me
about his visit to a cemetery outside Washington, DC, where
the wife of Henry Adams, the nineteenth-century historian, is
buried. He was startled to see a statue of a mysterious, hooded
figure carved on the top of her tombstone.

"I was haunted by that image and couldn't shake it from
my mind. I did some research and found out that Henry Adams's wife had killed herself at a young age. He had commis-
sioned that statue for her grave. You can't tell who it is or what
it means, but I don't think it's her; I think it's death. It stands
for the unanswered questions he had about her suicide. The
questions all of us have who go through this experience."

According to Jewish custom, there is a one-year waiting
period between the time a person is buried and when his or
her grave marking is unveiled. Twelve months after Harry's
death, on another cold, bright December day, I stood in front

of my husband's tombstone and read the words I had chosen after much soul-searching: "Harry Federico José Reiss, M.D. January 12, 1946–December 16, 1989. Physician and Healer. In Peace, Love and Serenity."

The wish for "Peace, Love and Serenity" was my prayer for both of us. Although Harry was now safely laid to rest, I was just beginning my painful journey toward understanding and acceptance of the reasons why he had chosen to die. In the aftermath of the chaos that his suicide left behind, I had to make sense of his death in order to reclaim not only my future but also my past.

$\mathcal{C\!\!R}$ 5

The Stigma

"There is nothing romantic about this journey."

—Mariette Hartley

A year after Harry killed himself, my disastrous financial circumstances necessitated my getting a part-time job to supplement my writer's income. The first week I was there, a group of women who worked at the organization invited me out to lunch. "So tell us all about yourself," one of them began. "Are you married? Single?" I froze, totally unprepared for how to answer her question.

"I was married," I stammered my reply.

"Oh?" she continued. "How long has it been since your divorce?"

"No, it's not that." I was finally able to collect myself. "My husband died."

There was a long silence at the table. Then, the same woman said to me in a sympathetic hush, "I'm sorry. I thought you were one of us."

Her words cut through me like a knife. If my new coworkers considered me an outsider because I was a young widow, what would they think if they knew my husband had killed himself? Panic swept over me; I wanted to run out of the restaurant.

"How old was your husband?" another woman asked.

"Forty-three." I could hear myself talking from a distance, as if I were dead myself.

"Do you mind if I ask how he died?" the interrogation continued.

"Of course not," I replied, hoping they would mistake my almost paralyzing distress for conventional grief. I launched into a detailed story, describing how Harry had suffered a heart attack from working too hard. How he had exhausted himself taking care of his dying parents. How he was slightly overweight. I even added the facts that heart disease ran in his family, that his cholesterol was high.

I recounted entering into his office to find him slumped over his desk. Calling 911. Watching the police and paramedics trying to save him. The medical examiner pronouncing him dead. Although the framework of the narrative remained intact, the facts were reshaped for my comfort. The women listened supportively, yet with intense curiosity.

This was my standard explanation of Harry's premature and sudden death. I told variations of this story to his patients, our neighbors, my relatives, the doctors with whom he worked, his secretary, our casual friends. I was convinced that I had no other recourse but to deny the truth: If I had failed to keep my husband alive, the least I could do was to protect his name and reputation by lying about his decision to kill himself.

A few weeks after that calamitous lunch with my coworkers, I found myself on the elevator with the woman who had asked me about my marital status. She started telling me about the unexpected death of a board member, which had occurred the day before. It was a massive heart attack, she confided. All of a sudden, she gasped. "I'm so sorry," she apologized. "How insensitive of me. Please forgive me."

For the life of me, I could not understand what she was talking about. Why should I be upset that this person had died? Awkward silence filled the elevator as the woman looked away in embarrassment. I racked my brain trying to figure out what possibly could be wrong. Then, I remembered. "That's right," I blurted out. "My husband died of a heart attack."

I felt humiliated by my inappropriate response. At that moment, I realized how dramatically my life had become transformed by the stigma that surrounds suicide. Why should I have to cover up what had happened? Yet, I also knew that if I decided to be honest with my colleague in the elevator, the *real* reason for my husband's death would be broadcast throughout the office by the end of the day. Even though part of me wanted to tell her the truth, I was convinced that it was none of her business. The boundary between my right to privacy and the shame I felt at hiding my secret had totally blurred.

"My boyfriend and I broke up shortly after I told him about my sister's suicide," says Karen, a student at the University of Alabama. "I'll never know if it was related, but he had a hard time with her death. He asked me all these questions, like if suicide ran in my family and did I have problems with my parents. As he turned away from me, I began to feel tainted, like something must really be wrong with me."

Dr. Edward Dunne, an editor of *Suicide and Its Aftermath: Understanding and Counseling the Survivors*, is a highly regarded clinical psychologist and a suicide survivor himself. He believes that the stigma of suicide is so powerful because people who kill themselves are breaking an unwritten contract that declares we should not be free to leave society at will.

"The whole horror of suicide resonates with the most profound existential question of one's life: 'Why should I live?' " he explains. "To hear that someone has answered no, that someone has *broken the rules*, is extraordinarily threatening to survivors."

In 1973, Dr. Dunne's sixteen-year-old brother, Tim, committed suicide by jumping in front of a train. Dr. Dunne, who was fourteen years older than Tim, was in private practice in New York when his brother killed himself.

"My mourning was compounded both as a brother and as a professional," he told me. "Being a psychologist in your family is like being a lifeguard in a hurricane. My mother and sisters were both nurses, with specialities in mental health counseling. At that time, there was an institutional belief that suicides did not occur in a therapist's family. Nobody in the mental health community talked about the subject openly.

"I found out about my brother when I was in the middle of conducting a group therapy session. I got called out and I left the group. Part of my experience of being a survivor is the ability to remember many of the seemingly inconsequential details which surround the event. Twenty-two years later, I remember who was in the group at that time. Even now, I can visualize their faces when this unprecedented event of having the group interrupted took place.

"Although I believe that I saw most of the group members only a few more times, I still remember who they were and what they were wearing at the time. What I don't remember is who in my family called me. Who told me the news? The receptionist had simply said that there was a 'family emergency.' She handed me the phone and I was told. But I don't know by whom.

"I had always liked to believe that I was in control but, even at that early point, my mind was involved in constructing its own version of the story, holding onto details here, deciding to let go of others. It was as if I was just the body helping the mind get from place to place, person to person, as this drama unfolded.

"Tim's suicide was written up in the newspapers so I didn't lie to people who knew him. But we hardly talked about my brother when our family got together. My father was never able to acknowledge my brother's death as a suicide. I thought it was my job to make him do so, so I bugged him with the 'truth' for years afterward. Why could he not see? What was the point of holding on to the illusion that something else had happened? Our later conversations were characterized by a familiar pattern of avoidance, and they would leave me frustrated and infuriated.

"The conflict kept us apart in his last years, and robbed us of the opportunity to talk about my brother at all. Years later, seeing so many families in the same situation—he says 'yes,' she says 'no,'; she says 'deliberate,' he says 'accident'; he says 'suicide,' she says 'murder'—I recognize that I was not allowing my father his own personal path to grief and recovery. I wanted him on mine. Now I would welcome the chance to tell him that he had a right to his own version of this story, to his own grief. Certainly there was enough grief to go around. Would he have come to my path if I had let him find his own way? Of course, I have no way of knowing.

"Seven years after Tim's suicide, at my sister's suggestion, we formed a group of mental health professionals who were survivors of suicide. When I got to the first group meeting, I had the feeling that we were all somehow criminals of some sort—meeting secretly on a Saturday in an otherwise closed university. The group lasted four years and it was very powerful because we all shared this secret. As professionals, we felt that we should have been savvy enough to see it coming. In other words, it brought up—would I send a suicidal patient to you? How could you help someone if you couldn't even help your own flesh and blood? If we told the truth, would it be the end of any referrals we might get from other professionals? There is very little written for therapists on how to deal with the suicide of a client: We can only go so far in making sure that our patients live. Dealing with the suicide of a loved one complicates the situation even more.

"I have learned the importance of respecting everyone's grieving as unique to them and am encouraged that the survivor group movement has also made this discovery. We are more humble than in the beginning. Now we know that there are no true prescriptions. No one path. We tell you what our path has been. Then it is up to you."

The stigma of suicide presents us with a profound dilemma: whether to tell the truth in order to prove that we are not ashamed, even though, by being honest, we might be ostracized by society. "Because my husband's suicide was covered extensively in the local papers and on the television news, I became a pariah in an instant," recalls Marie, the widow of the California politician. "Everyone was looking for the skeletons in his closet and I could have been one of them. My heart aches for Lisa Foster, the wife of President Clinton's former deputy White House counsel, Vincent Foster, who shot himself several years after my husband committed suicide. All these powerful men down in Washington sitting around spending taxpayers's money to try to figure out why he did it and even *if* he did it. They can hold investigative hearings forever as far as I'm concerned but they will never find the answer to his suicide. At least an answer that makes any kind of sense. That is the cruelty of suicide: We will never know what they were thinking when they pulled the trigger or swallowed the pills or jumped out the window. We will never have closure on their deaths.

"I was immediately cast out from my social circle. It was as if my friends buried me along with my husband. I had a friend call me and say, 'I feel very ambivalent about Tony's suicide.' Well, I didn't have the luxury to feel ambivalent—I had to deal with the huge mess that his death left behind. By one act, my husband not only ended his life but also ended my world.

"I have a hard time telling people whom I don't know about Tony's suicide. I feel like I'm damaged goods. Two years after Tony died, I went on a cruise. The first evening I was seated at the captain's table. During the get-acquainted conversation, someone asked me why I was traveling alone. I replied that my husband had passed away. Then, another person asked the inevitable How? a socially acceptable question, as I have quickly discovered. I decided to tell the truth and answered that my husband had killed himself. It was like that E. F. Hutton commercial where everyone drops their forks and stops talking. There was this total silence and then the subject was instantly changed. I decided to go back to 'heart attack' when asked about my husband's death; it was just easier.

"When a person you love kills himself, suicide is put on your menu. It becomes a permanent part of your life. I worry about my children. When they get upset, like teenagers do, I'm terrified that they might want to kill themselves. They're also very traumatized by Tony's suicide and I know it has entered their mindframes like it has mine. For that reason alone, I'm furious at Tony and can never forgive him for what he has done."

The idea that suicide is a family legacy or "curse" intensifies the stigma of suicide, especially for children. Jessica was three months pregnant with her father's first grandchild when he jumped off the roof of a downtown Chicago skyscraper. She almost lost the baby from the trauma and blames her father for her difficult pregnancy and birth. "My father's suicide will always cast a cloud over my daughter's life because she will never know if suicide can be inherited," she states. "If it can, she will wonder if she was born with the same gene that killed her grandfather; if it's not, she will ask why he didn't want to stick around to see her born."

Dr. Dunne strongly believes that children, even very young ones, should be told the truth about suicide from the very beginning. "It is unrealistic to hide the fact of suicide from children," he emphasizes. "Children eventually find out the truth and often under circumstances where they are given little support, like hearing the news from a schoolmate or a relative, for example. Children can pick up overtones in a family and can sense when something is not quite right. Why betray the trust of children when they've already been betrayed by one adult? Children should learn from the experience that not all adults will abandon you or let you down."

In a recent article on censorship in school libraries and the classroom, *The New York Times* reported: "Most would-be censors object to the obvious 's' words—sex, suicide, Satanism and swearing." For survivors, "s" also stands for stigma, shame, and silence. Even though suicide is not our decision, our lives are irreversibly affected by its consequences.

"There was always a sense of confusion and loss when I was growing up," remembers John, a sixty-four-year-old writer from San Francisco who discovered at the age of fifty that his father had killed himself when John was five months old. "The real puzzlement is that I will never know if learning about my father's suicide earlier would have made a difference in my outlook. I think it would have, because I have lived most of my life in the shadowlands—not quite telling the truth. With my first wife, I would have affairs and never be quite honest. It was because I felt comfortable living in a secret world, similar to the one I grew up in. Since knowing about my father, I feel freer about being honest instead of lying.

"My father was a lawyer and was twenty-five years old when he died. My mother remarried when I was two, to a man who had three sons, much older than I. My stepfather adopted me and I took his name. My mother told me that my father had died from a heart attack but she never said anything else about him. When I was four or five, I started picking up that something was wrong. We never visited my father's gravesite, there were no photographs of him, I never met any of his family—I didn't know my grandparents, aunts, uncles, or cousins. My mother said that his parents were angry at her but she never explained why.

"Throughout my childhood and adolescence, I knew intuitively that there was something different about my father's death. I began to wonder if my father had ever actually existed. When I was twenty, I started therapy. I tried reasoning with my mother to tell me what had really happened to my father. She became furious. 'I don't want to talk about it,' she would scream at me. 'Stop bothering me.' I was convinced that I was illegitimate; suicide never even entered my mind.

"When I turned fifty, I decided to hire a private detective to find out the real truth. The detective located my father's death certificate, which said that the cause of death was asphyxiation by gas. He then found out where my father was buried. I went to the cemetery. His tombstone said: 'Beloved Father and Son.' It did not say, 'Husband.' Obviously, my grandparents had buried him. I confronted my mother. I told her that I believed my father had killed himself and I wanted to know if it was true and why.

"My mother finally admitted that my father had committed suicide by putting his head in the oven. She said he did it because the Mafia was after him for gambling debts. I knew she was lying but she wouldn't change her story. Then I asked her if my stepbrothers and stepfather had known about his suicide all along and she said yes. I felt totally betrayed that I had grown up in a family with everyone knowing something and my not knowing it. I only knew that something was wrong but not *what* was wrong.

"I decided not to pursue my father's death any longer. I didn't make an attempt to locate my father's relatives. I did ask my stepbrothers, however, why they never said anything to me about my father's suicide, and they explained that they felt it wasn't their place to tell me.

"My mother died the next year. She left me a battered suitcase with my father's name on it. It was totally empty. She also left me a bunch of photographs. There was only one of my father, and I was stunned to see how much I looked like him. I was furious at my mother because she withheld so much from me about my father.

"I lived with a lie until I turned fifty; my mother lived with a lie her entire life. She was torn apart by a secret that affected every part of her existence. Suicide is such a stigma that we feel we have to bury it. It was as if my mother had committed a murder that she didn't want anyone to find out about. I used to be so angry at her. Now, I see how guilt and shame, especially when hidden, can control your whole life. I feel so sad for all of us—for my mother, my father, and myself."

Suicide is not a topic that is openly discussed. It is a stain that blemishes the illusion of normalcy and our desire to demonstrate that we are like everyone else. Helen, seventy-four, a retired school principal living in Orlando, Florida, believes that suicide is a disgrace that trespasses on the accepted standards of society. Her nephew crashed his small plane in the woods eight months ago, leaving a note saying that he did not want to live after losing his job as an automobile executive. Helen admits that she is very uncomfortable discussing his story.

"I have always believed that you should keep your family secrets private," she states. "People who kill themselves let out their confusions publicly instead of keeping their problems to themselves. Their actions are outside the accepted code of behavior, especially for someone in my generation. Suicide is a disgrace because all religions frown on it. It is considered murder, taking a life. I think suicide is rational and very planned; it is not impulsive. We have all had thoughts of suicide at one time or another, myself included. But there's a certain resilience in the human spirit that wants to live. If I can overcome my feelings of despair, others should be able to do so also."

The taboo against suicide can often condemn us to a life sentence of silence, like John's mother, who hid her secret from her son, and Gina, who cannot even feel safe talking to her therapist about her husband's shooting himself before her eyes. Yet, when we finally begin to discuss suicide openly, there is a certain relief. We no longer fear being exposed, because we are in control of our own history.

"I never told anyone about my mother's suicide until last year, not even my husband or children," says Annie, a forty-year-old physician practicing in a hospital in suburban Indianapolis. "When I was sixteen, my mother drove her car off a bridge and drowned. I invented a story that I never deviated from: My mother had been killed in a car accident when I was five and I couldn't remember anything about it. I never varied any of the details so I was never caught in the lie. If you live with a lie for your whole life, you almost come to believe it.

"I was brought up in a Catholic background. I lived in a small town in New Hampshire and my parents divorced when I was five, which was very unusual. I went to live with my father's mother, and my mother moved to a nearby town with my two-year-old sister.

"My mother never recovered from the divorce. She was always depressed and unhappy. I hardly ever saw her, even though we lived so close. Two months before she killed herself, she took an overdose of antidepressants and was hospitalized for six weeks. Two weeks after being released from the hospital, she drove her car off the bridge. I never knew any of this. My grandmother wouldn't tell me any of the details of my mother's death, just that she had died in a car accident. My grandmother wouldn't even let me go to the funeral—it was weird, I went to school the day my mother was buried.

"Somehow I knew something was wrong. Why wasn't I allowed to go to my own mother's funeral? I went to see my uncle, who told me that the police had determined that my mother's accident was deliberate. He said that she had not been buried in the Catholic cemetery and her coffin had not been allowed in the church.

"A few days later, the local newspaper ran a story on the front page with the headline CAR ACCIDENT RULED SUICIDE. It included all the gory details about my mother's suicide. I was humiliated because everyone in town now knew my business. My friends shunned me and even crossed the street when they saw me. I felt alienated from everything that was once so familiar. My grandmother told me that suffering makes you a better person because it allows you to live through a new experience. But I don't believe that for a second. As soon as I graduated high school, I moved to Boston. I put myself through college and medical school and never once returned to my hometown. When my grandmother and sister wanted to see me, they had to come to Boston.

"I married my husband in medical school. We had children right away and our sons are now ten and twelve. Two years ago, I began to suffer from a terrible depression. I later made the connection that this was the age when my mother killed herself, but, at the time, I wasn't consciously thinking of her. My depression became crippling and the chief of medical services at the hospital suggested that I go for help. I was very reluctant to go for therapy, but I got the feeling that if I didn't make the attempt, my job would be in jeopardy.

"I was in therapy for six months before I told my therapist about my mother. She was the first person I ever told. I couldn't stop crying and she asked me if I thought suicide was wrong. I said, no, of course not. I'm a physician who often treats terminally ill patients. I know that many times the families of these patients will help them to die. This doesn't bother me at all because I know they're trying to help end the suffering. It's different with my mother. She killed herself because she thought she was a failure, both as a wife and as a mother.

But before she drove off that bridge, she should have thought of her children. I don't blame her; I miss her. I miss having a mother.

"My husband was very supportive when I told him the truth about my mother, although I think he was hurt that I had kept such an important part of my life hidden from him. I still haven't been able to tell my sons. I don't want them to think any less of their grandmother. I've started talking to select people about my mother's suicide, trying out how it feels to be honest. I'm still very wary, however, because I've noticed that most people recoil at the subject and are very uncomfortable discussing it.

"I care for several patients with AIDS. They get very upset when people ask them how they became sick. I can really identify with them because I feel the same sense of accusation from people when they ask me how my mother died. As if the *how* defines your life. There is a similar stigma attached to AIDS. It's as if you have somehow brought on your situation yourself so you shouldn't expect any sympathy or compassion from others."

It is very distressing for suicide survivors that the *how* of our loved one's deaths, as Annie describes it, comes to represent the sum total of their lives. Even as we move cautiously to reveal the truth about their suicides, we still remain defensive about their decision to take their own lives.

"Although I don't lie about my sister's suicide, I immediately add that she graduated second in her class at Stanford Law," explains Pete, a salesman from Salt Lake City. "It's almost like saying that my sister wasn't a nut or some mentally unstable person who couldn't function. I feel that I have to somehow validate her life because her death is considered so perverse and unnatural."

Even though it is difficult for survivors to accept the truth about our loved one's suicide, it is even more painful to expose our shame to other people. "I was determined to erase any evidence that my daughter had shot herself," explains Connie, a forty-four-year-old advertising executive from St. Louis. "Three years ago, when my daughter was home on spring break from her freshman year of college, she lay down on her bed, put my husband's gun to her temple, and pulled the trigger. I had no idea that anything was bothering her. Her blood-soaked bedroom reflected the carnage I felt in my soul; everything I once knew was hurled out of place.

"I hired professional cleaners to clean her bedroom. I also had them remove her bed. When they finished, I examined the room inch by inch. After searching for several hours, I found some blood spots on the wall that they had missed. I was desperately searching for evidence. I cleaned the spots because I didn't want neighbors or relatives to gawk at the signs of destruction and say, 'So, this is what happened.' I kept on searching and finally discovered the hole in the ceiling where the police had removed the bullet. I said, 'Aha, I found it.' I knew there was something there for me.

"At least the bullet hole was a connection to her, as horrible as it was. I brought a stepladder from the kitchen, found some ready-made plaster and a spatula in the tool closet, and filled up the hole. I smoothed it down and painted it over. I felt as if I were protecting my daughter. No one has a right to make a spectacle of the situation, even though she did not have the right to do what she did.

"Except for the space where her bed had been, her bedroom looked normal again. It seemed so safe and sunny. That was all I wanted—for everything to be normal, like it used to be."

For those of us who have survived the suicide of a loved one, life will never be normal again. We have changed and will never be the same people we once were. Yet, as we become more open about our experiences, the stigma of suicide will start to recede. By letting go of the secret of our loved one's death, we can begin to reclaim our memories of his or her life.

Part Three

THE AFTERMATH

℘ 6

The Blame and Guilt:
Searching for the Whys

"We do not believe in ascribing 'responsibility' for
suicide to anyone other than the victim. The failure
to choose life is the failure of the deceased, not of
the survivor."

—Edward Dunne and Karen Dunne-Maxim,
Suicide and Its Aftermath: Understanding and Counseling the Survivors

Two years after Harry's suicide, my cousin Adam called to tell me that our Uncle Sam had died at the age of ninety-seven. My sadness at the news was tempered by the knowledge that Sam's long life had been filled with much happiness and many accomplishments. The funeral was to be held at the same cemetery in Massachusetts where my father and Harry are buried, and Adam asked if I needed a ride.

"I'm surprised you're going to the funeral," I remarked.

"Why wouldn't I?" he replied, confused by the bitterness of my tone. "Sam was the last of his generation. He was the patriarch of the family."

"You didn't come to Harry's," I stated. Although we had discussed Harry's suicide, Adam had never offered me an explanation for not attending the funeral.

"That was different, Carla," he answered. "You of all people should be able to understand that."

What did I understand? I understood that Adam's confusion and discomfort at Harry's decision to kill himself prevented him from paying his last respects to a man he had known for more than twenty years. I understood that he was angry and ambivalent about Harry's suicide. But, most of all, I understood that his lack of support for me on the day I buried my husband had served to compound and validate my own profound feelings of guilt and blame for Harry's death.

Sigmund Freud, commenting on a friend who had hanged himself, made the following observation: "What drove him to it? As an explanation, the world is ready to hurl the most ghastly accusations at the unfortunate widow." The presumption of guilt directed at suicide survivors by society is devastating; yet, unfortunately, we are often our own severest judges. Why didn't we see that our loved ones were depressed? Why didn't we force them to get help? Why didn't we return their last telephone call? Why did we say such terrible things to them during that last argument? The decision to commit suicide creates a sense of utter helplessness for those of us who are left behind. In order to maintain a sense of control, we often blame the deaths of our loved ones on actions *we* took or omissions *we* made.

"My son killed himself two months ago with a rifle I bought him for his sixteenth birthday," says Craig, a forty-two-year-old mechanic from a small town in Idaho. "He had been upset because he didn't make the football team at school and I thought the gun would cheer him up because he loves to hunt. Instead, he took it into the woods and used it to blow his head off. It never entered my mind that my son was thinking of killing himself. He had been moody and withdrawn, but I just assumed he was acting like a typical teenager. Now I ask myself over and over: What would have happened if I hadn't given him the gun? Would my son still be alive?"

While Craig torments himself with the notion that his purchase of a gun precipitated his son's death, Priscilla, a fifty-eight-year-old college professor from Madison, Wisconsin, blames her father's suicide on her insistence that he seek professional help for his deepening depression.

"My father was almost immobilized after the death of my mother," she says. "For months afterward, he rarely left the house and practically stopped eating. He even gave his cat away to a neighbor. I knew that I couldn't help him all by myself and pleaded with him to see a doctor. He resisted, saying that at the age of eighty-one he was not about to tell his private business to a complete stranger. I begged him to go at least once—for my sake—and he finally agreed.

"I found a psychiatrist who specialized in treating depression in elderly people. On the morning of my father's first appointment, I canceled my classes so I could accompany him to the doctor's office. When I went to his house to pick him up, I found his body hanging in the hallway closet. I remember thinking, This is my fault, this is my fault. My father must have been so terrified at the idea of facing his ghosts that he panicked. I will never know if he would eventually have gotten better on his own or if I pushed him to his death by forcing him to go for help. All I know is that I loved him and thought I was doing what was best for him."

Even though Priscilla realized that her father was depressed and tried to get him professional counseling, she was ultimately incapable of stopping him from taking his life. Other survivors blame themselves for failing to recognize what they believe must have been obvious warning signs.

"My best friend shot himself after spending the evening with me watching a basketball game," says Frank, a thirty-year-old journalist from New Orleans. "He had recently separated from his wife and all night he talked about how much he missed his kids. I knew he was sad, but he never said anything about dying. How could I have been so stupid not to have seen what was going on?"

It is extremely painful for suicide survivors to reconstruct the factors in our loved ones' lives that might have influenced their decision to commit suicide. "I had absolutely no idea why my brother would want to kill himself," recounts Hugh, a fifty-seven-year-old lawyer from Atlanta. "We talked about everything, and I considered him my best friend. Last year, he was killed instantly when his car crashed into a tree. I just assumed, like everyone else, that it had been a tragic accident. Two days later, I received a letter from him mailed on the day he died. He said he was sorry for what he was going to do but could see no other way out. He explained that he owed hundreds of thousands of dollars in gambling debts and was very afraid. He asked me to pray for him.

"I was devastated that my brother did not come to me for help before he decided to kill himself. But I also felt duped: I had absolutely no idea about his gambling problem. If my brother had really died in a car accident, I would have buried him in peace without looking back. Instead, I acted as if I were a detective investigating a murder rather than a man who was grieving for his brother: I talked to his friends and business associates; I went through his apartment with a fine-tooth comb. I found out details about his life that I really didn't want to know about. We all have parts of our lives that we keep to ourselves and don't share with anyone else; suicide reveals a person's innermost secrets for the whole world to see."

For survivors, sometimes even being able to identify the reasons for a loved one's suicide is not enough to alleviate their confusion and self-doubt. "My wife was a functioning depressive who constantly talked about killing herself," explains Greg, a thirty-six-year-old engineer from a small city in Mississippi. "She was always looking to feel better, always looking for a cure. She went to different doctors, took all the new pills on the market, read all the articles on depression that she could find. Nothing seemed to help. Eleven months ago, she went into our garage and turned on the engine of the car. I found her when I came home from a drive with our two sons. I know the *why* of her death but it doesn't make it any easier. I can't accept that nothing can be done for someone like my wife—she wanted to live but her sadness just overwhelmed her."

Not only do survivors feel powerless and inadequate in the face of suicide, we also feel hurt and betrayed by our loved ones for making such an irrevocable decision without consulting us or turning to us for help. "I thought my husband and I shared everything with each other, but obviously I was wrong," says Claire, a sixty-eight-year-old grandmother who lives in a suburb of Cincinnati. "Three years ago, on the day after our thirty-ninth wedding anniversary, my husband killed himself by taking a bottle of sleeping pills and then putting a plastic bag over his head. His suicide forced me to reevaluate not only my entire marriage but also my whole life.

"My husband had suffered a stroke the year before his suicide. At that time, we decided that it would be best if he sell his business and retire. His recovery was very successful and he had regained most of his speech and motor abilities.

Our sex life had been affected, though, and I guess there must have been other areas where he was having problems. But he never talked about how he was feeling. He always acted cheerful and optimistic—at least with me.

"After my husband's funeral, I found a copy of *Final Exit* in his bureau drawer. It was like a cookbook filled with detailed recipes for death. At first, I blamed the book for his suicide; then, I realized that my husband must have been making plans to kill himself for a long time. I started wondering what else I didn't know about this man with whom I had shared almost half a century of my life. His suicide threw my whole world into question; I no longer know what to believe in or whom to trust."

As Claire discovered, it is not books and doctors that kill people: Suicide is self-murder. To survivors, this is more agonizing then the barbiturate recipes in *Final Exit* or the suicide machines of Dr. Kevorkian. We tell ourselves that our mothers hanged themselves because they were losing their memories, our sons shot themselves because their girlfriends broke up with them, our wives jumped from the balcony because we told them we were leaving, our brothers swallowed sleeping pills because they had AIDS. But we know that most people in similar circumstances do not kill themselves—why them?

Society is uncomfortable speaking ill of the dead; as a result, the underlying motives for suicide are often attributed to anyone, anything, other than the people who have killed themselves. Because we already feel guilty for having failed to save our loved ones, survivors are vulnerable to the accusations and finger-pointing that are so often directed at us after a suicide.

"My daughter's death was so public," says Denise, a fifty-year-old psychologist from Toronto. "We were arguing about her decision to drop out of college when she suddenly ran to the balcony and jumped. Her body landed on top of a car parked in front of our apartment building. I remember racing down eight flights of stairs as if I were in a dream. The police came and we had to wait around until the medical examiner arrived. By then, a whole crowd had gathered. I heard some-one make a joke about the owner of the car; it was such a sad, undignified end for my daughter.

"Her death was reported in the newspaper, with the article quoting a neighbor as saying that she had heard screaming in the apartment right before my daughter jumped. I felt so ex-posed. The whole spotlight of my daughter's suicide immedi-ately focused on me: What kind of mother was I? What had I said to her to make her want to kill herself? I even became paranoid that some people actually thought I might have pushed her off the balcony. My own guilt was so immense that I accepted the judgment that my daughter's suicide meant something was wrong with me, not her. Now, after three years of intensive therapy, I have finally started to forgive myself for her death. Mothers and daughters fight all the time; I loved her with my soul, but it was her decision, not mine, to die."

For a suicide survivor, even a casual remark can cause great guilt and remorse. "My best friend killed herself twenty-seven years ago and there is still a part of me that believes I contributed to her death," says Betty, a housewife from Rapid City, South Dakota. "We were both thirty-three years old and were pregnant together. We gave birth within one week of each other. She was my oldest friend—we had known each other since kindergarten.

"My friend and her husband were trying to buy a house but they were having money problems. They had two chil-dren and she was pregnant with the third when they were forced to move back to her parents' house. All during her pregnancy, she kept on talking about their cramped living arrangements. I once said to her, 'I can't believe what you're going through. If I were you, I would probably put my head in the oven.' After the birth of her baby, she went into a postpartum depression. She lay in bed with the blinds drawn. I would visit her but she barely spoke to me. She went to a doctor who gave her some pills, but nothing seemed to work.

"When the baby was six months old, my friend committed suicide by putting her head in the oven. She left notes to her mother, her husband, and her children. There was no mention of me in any of the notes. I was convinced that I had given her the idea to kill herself and I was devastated. Even now, I still feel guilty that my flippant remark might have influenced her decision to kill herself. Her funeral was awful; her mother was totally distraught yet angry at the same time. She kept on calling out, 'Why did you do this to me?' Her husband virtually abandoned the family, and her parents ended up raising the children.

"There were six of us who were best friends and now there were five. We talked about how we had failed her, how we could have helped her more. We wondered if we should have 'intruded' ourselves into her life, instead of not interfering with what was going on. Her family would sometimes say she didn't want to see us because she wasn't feeling well. It's really difficult to know what is support and what is intrusion.

"I feel a great sense of waste: My friend could have been a wonderful mother and person. Her death has made me more aware of how I speak. I keep coming back to how insensitive I must have sounded to her. But I have also come to believe that you can't stop what is going to take place if a person's mind is made up. There is no way to force your way in; the only way you can make a difference is if you are asked to be part of the decision."

Some survivors experience a sense of relief when a suicide

ends the physical or mental suffering of a loved one. Yet, even this understanding is often accompanied by feelings of guilt and blame on the part of the person who is left behind.

"My mother committed suicide because she didn't want to be a burden to anyone," explains Hazel, a fifty-five-year-old teacher from Newark, New Jersey. "She had been suffering from severe arthritis for many years and was becoming increasingly dependent on me for her needs. Six months after her eighty-third birthday, she swallowed a bottle of painkillers. Although that was five years ago, I still feel I could have done more to help her. I also worry that I might have been giving her signals that I was becoming resentful about having to care for her, that I was so involved with my own life I was unable to see her increasing suffering.

"I remember one night several weeks before she killed herself. She called me to say that she was in a lot of pain. I told her to take a Valium. In the morning, I phoned her to see how she was doing. She said she was feeling better and apologized for disturbing me. When I reconstruct that event, I always feel guilty. My mother was very stoic and hardly ever complained. I should have seen that her call was a cry for help and driven over to her apartment—it was only fifteen minutes away. But I just went to sleep.

"Although I was my mother's primary caretaker, I did not have the keys to her apartment. It was as if she always wanted to keep her independence. Besides, if something was wrong I knew I could get her keys from the building superintendent. My mother and I went out to lunch on the day she committed suicide. Afterward, she handed me a set of keys to her apartment. I thought it was a little strange but I didn't say anything to her. I remembered her telephone call in the night and just assumed that she was beginning to feel more vulnerable.

"When I took her home, my mother made me try out the

keys to make sure they worked. She was very insistent about it. The next day, I called her first thing in the morning like I always did and there was no answer. I tried not to worry, but by mid-morning I started to become very afraid when she didn't answer her phone. I drove over to her apartment on my lunch break. I took her freshly minted keys from my pocketbook to open her door. That's when I knew something was dreadfully wrong. I walked into her bedroom. My mother was lying on her bed fully dressed with her shoes on—she was wearing the same outfit she had worn to lunch the day before. There was a key for her safety deposit box taped to her jewelry box. There was an envelope with $200 in it, labeled 'petty cash.' At first, I thought she had died of a stroke or heart attack. I was not thinking suicide. Then, I checked the pill bottles on her bureau. When I saw that they were all empty, I knew she had killed herself.

"The worst part about suicide is that all the attention is on the last minutes and days, not the years that came before. In my mother's case, there were eighty-three years of a rich history before she killed herself. But her suicide dominates my memories of her. I regret that I didn't have the chance to talk her out of doing it. I wonder what would have happened if I had followed my initial instincts to ask her what was wrong when she gave me the keys to her apartment. I imagine that she took the pills as soon as I left her. Therefore, if I had come right back, I might have been able to save her. It's the not knowing that gnaws at me all the time."

Because the solution to the puzzle of suicide lies exclusively with the people who have killed themselves, rational explanations and logical conclusions are of little comfort to survivors. We are unsettled and confused in grieving for the very person who has taken our loved one's life. Guilt and blame serve to offer us a context for our mourning, connecting us to the experience of death by including us in the process.

After Harry died, my life was consumed with finding reasons for his suicide. I faulted the medical establishment for not recognizing that one of their own was struggling with depression. I blamed his brother for not putting aside his wounded pride to console Harry after their father's death. I accused his friends of abandoning him as he visibly started to disassemble. Most of all, I blamed myself: It seemed inconceivable that my life force had not been strong enough to keep both of us alive.

Several months ago, the elderly mother of my neighbor, Sandy, died from heart failure. When I called to offer my condolences, Sandy began crying. "All my relatives are blaming me for her death," she sobbed. "Three weeks ago, my mother had an operation on her knee. She never recovered and died while still in the hospital. Now, everyone is saying I shouldn't have allowed such major surgery to be performed on such an old woman. But my mother was in agony and told me she couldn't continue living in such pain."

"It wasn't your fault, Sandy," I told her. "You have to forget about what others are saying. You know you made the best decision for your mother under the circumstances. You are not guilty for her death. That would be too easy."

My words to Sandy were shaped by my own arduous journey. Even though her mother had died from natural causes, while my husband's death was self-inflicted, neither Sandy nor I were to blame. Harry did not ask either my permission or my blessing. In order to forgive not only him but also myself, I had to accept that, ultimately, it was Harry's own choice to kill himself. All I can do is disagree with his decision.

The Helplessness:
Haunted by the What-Ifs

"Suicide is a permanent solution to a
temporary problem."

—Common adage

The movie audience burst into applause as the despondent man, stirred by the impassioned pleas of his distraught wife, removed the loaded revolver from his mouth. Maybe it was true, I thought, suddenly flooded with doubts. With the right words, the right gestures, it is possible to vanquish the hopeless desperation of a person you love. Unlike the star of the picture, however, I had not been able to save my husband's life. What if I had said something different to Harry?

What if I had been able to reach him? What if I had acted more sensitively, more aggressively?

"You are my lifeline," Harry used to tell me during those last terrible months. "You are the only reason I am staying alive." And, still believing in the popular myth that love conquers all and that it is possible to infuse our will to live into another person, I initially accepted the responsibility—and, ultimate failure—for Harry's suicide. By convincing myself that an action or word on my part would have prevented his death, I did not have to admit that my husband's decision to end his life was both solitary and unconnected to me.

Like most survivors, I was haunted by the infinite regrets that are woven into the fabric of suicide. I would replay the chronology of events leading up to Harry's death, searching for lost opportunities to reverse the inevitable outcome. Only as I began to accept the idea that my husband's choice to kill himself was his alone did the powerful grip of the what-ifs of his suicide begin to loosen. Gradually, I came to understand that while it might be possible to help someone whose fear is death, there are no guarantees for a person whose fear is life.

"I made up tricks to keep my son alive," relates Molly, a seventy-eight-year-old retired office manager from New Haven, Connecticut. "He was diagnosed as a manic-depressive when he was a teenager, shortly after my husband died. Seventeen years ago, at the age of twenty-five, he finally succeeded in committing suicide after many previous attempts. I was always trying to convince him not to kill himself, reminding him that you never know what is on the other side. I would tell him that he should try to fix what was bothering him, not to give up.

"When my son was nineteen, he took an overdose of pills, then cut his veins. I got a call from the police, who had found him in the middle of the street attempting to get run over.

After that, he was in and out of psychiatric hospitals. Over the years, he saw eleven psychiatrists and was on and off a whole array of medications. He was depressed most of the time, but when he was not in crisis he was a wonderful person.

"My life was dedicated to him. I was always terrified that he would kill himself. At one point, he dropped out of college and refused to go out of the house. Every night, I would drive home from work as fast as I could, afraid that I would come back to find him dead. Then, when I would see him waiting for me at the window, I would be relieved that he was alive. Once, I arrived home and found him unconscious in his bedroom. I picked him up and gave him coffee. He was a big man but I could lift him because of the adrenaline that was pumping through me. Another time he tried to jump out of the car while I was driving but I was able to stop him.

"I knew that my son was suicidal, but I always had the hope that it wouldn't happen. Friends would say that people who talk about killing themselves don't do it, but that isn't true. One day, I got tickets for a concert I thought he would enjoy. He didn't want to go, but for some reason I decided to go by myself. Usually, I didn't leave him alone at night. Before I left, I told him to watch a specific television program and to tell me about it when I came home. Somehow, I thought he would feel obligated not to kill himself if he had promised me something. I rushed home after the concert, scared, as always, that he might have taken his life when I was away.

"When I saw the light on in the garage, I knew immediately something was wrong. I opened the garage door and he was lying on the floor with his head in front of the exhaust pipe of the car. I started giving him mouth-to-mouth resuscitation. There were all these horrible sounds coming out of his chest. There was a door in the garage that led directly to the house. I ran in to call the police. There were fumes throughout the house. My son's dog, whom he adored, was dead in the living room. The house was filled with the urine and feces of the dog. I had noticed that my son's clothes were ripped, as if the dog had tried to save him by pulling him from the garage. It was January, so if the dog had been barking, none of the neighbors would have heard him because all the windows were closed.

"When the police came, I told them to take my son to a hospital. They said it was too late. His body was at the medical examiner's office for three days—I still remember every detail. After his suicide, I sold the house and moved away. I continued working but it felt dreamlike. I was functioning but not feeling anything.

"I finally went to a psychiatrist for help. I told him I could have done more to save my son. He told me I wasn't God, and I had saved him many times before. He said I had to remember I wasn't omnipotent. But the loss of a child is awful. A parent's death should come first. Although I had devoted my life to my son, I still felt in my heart that I didn't do enough for him because he died.

"One year after my son's suicide, I saw some children playing baseball in front of my house. One boy didn't want to play anymore. The other kids offered him the ball, extra points, anything to make him stay in the game. But he didn't want to play and went away. It reminded me of my son. I did everything I could to keep him here, but he wanted to go and he left.

"The only consolation I have is time. Although you never accept the idea, you learn to walk through life with the pain next to you. My son was a machine that broke. Even his dog had the natural instinct to live. In my life, I have suffered many losses—my husband, my parents, and my sister. But I still do not understand my son's death and I am a very old woman."

Most survivors share Molly's feelings of helplessness at not being able to keep someone alive, no matter how great their love or how much they care. "Three years ago, my brother's lover killed himself after he found out he was HIV positive," recounts Paula, a twenty-eight-year-old artist from San Francisco. "He was still very healthy but had lost a lot of friends to AIDS and didn't want to face the eventual suffering of that horrible disease. I was devastated because I knew he could have lived many years without being sick.

"Six months after his lover's suicide, my brother was diagnosed with HIV. I was terrified that he would also do something to himself. Before you experience suicide, you think it doesn't exist. It seems so remote and unreal until it happens to someone you know. My brother became very depressed. It was as if I were watching an accident taking place in front of my eyes. He went for counseling, joined a support group, even went to see a priest. I could see him going under but there was nothing I could do.

"On the first anniversary of his lover's death, my brother and I went for a long walk in the park. I asked him point-blank if he was feeling suicidal. He promised me he wasn't but I knew he was lying. That night, he took an overdose of sleeping pills. I keep asking myself what I could have done to save him. What if I had forced him to be admitted to the hospital? It feels as if I literally stood there and watched him die.

"Suicide is an act of violence, not only against yourself but also against others. There is such a sense of abandonment, of senselessness, of loss of the person. I guess we all carry around our own pain, although the pain that makes you kill yourself seems so cold and alien. Suicide is different. We each try to make peace with what exists outside of us, even though it's hard, but it's impossible to make peace with the darkness inside of us. Now, when I hear that someone is depressed or has received bad news, the first thing I think about is suicide. I can imagine anyone doing it, including myself."

As survivors reconstruct the deaths of our loved ones, we often identify key moments leading up to their suicides, moments when, we feel, we could have stopped the course of their actions.

"My sister slit her wrists after breaking up with her boyfriend," says Amanda, a twenty-three-year-old graduate student at the University of Iowa. "The night she died, there was a message from her on my answering machine asking me to call. I was tired and decided to phone back in the morning. I'll never know what would have happened if I had spoken to her. I keep thinking of her waiting for me and my just sleeping as she was bleeding to death in her bathtub."

Sometimes survivors react to their loved one's suicide with ambivalence and confusion, unsure if his or her death was truly self-inflicted or the result of a deadly accident or a tragic error. "Six years ago, my wife was killed when her car hit a tree in the curve of the road," says Simon, a thirty-three-year-old businessman from Grand Rapids, Michigan. "Several months before, she suffered a miscarriage and she had been terribly depressed since then. The police were unable to determine if her death was an accident or suicide. She didn't leave a note but she was always such a careful driver and she knew that stretch of road like the palm of her hand. It really bothers me to think that she planned her death. Then, I feel guilty because it shouldn't affect the way I think of her. She's gone and I miss her, period. The worst part is that I'll never find out the truth."

It is estimated that suicides represent 5 to 15 percent of all

fatal vehicular accidents. Doctors Mark Taff and Lauren Boglioli, in an April 1995 letter published in *The New York Times*,
explain that the criteria developed by medical examiners and
psychiatrists for determining vehicular suicide include: history
of psychiatric disease; previous suicide attempts; suicide note
or informing someone of suicide plans; single-vehicle collision
with a fixed roadside object; accelerator-pedal mark on the
shoe; absence of skid marks; witnessed acceleration into oncoming traffic; and use of drugs and alcohol. Yet, even the
most up-to-date use of scientific methodology cannot defini-
tively determine the true motivation of the person whose life
has been lost.

Suicide, by its very nature, leaves in its wake a tremendous
sense of confusion and displacement for those of us who have
been left behind. In the absence of conclusive evidence that a
suicide has taken place, survivors are forced to face even
greater feelings of uncertainty and ambiguity.

"My father just stopped eating after surgery," explains
Bruce, a sixty-two-year-old retired army captain from Virginia.
"I knew he was killing himself but I couldn't stop it. He just
lost his zest and slowly faded away in front of me. My sister
denies that he willed himself to die. She continues to believe
that he was sick and couldn't eat. But I consider his death self-
inflicted, a suicide. That's the only way I can deal with it."

For some survivors, the feeling of helplessness that pre-
cedes a loved one's decision to end his or her life is often
replaced by a sense of relief when the suicide finally occurs.
"When my mother killed herself eighteen years ago, it was as
if she had died and I was reborn," states Rosemarie, a thirty-
seven-year-old photographer from Boston. "My initial reaction
to her suicide was to move on with my life and not look back.
I was relieved that I no longer had to take care of her. My

mother suffered from periods of tremendous depression, and ever since I can remember, she was my responsibility. My parents divorced when I was ten. I was her only child, really her only friend. Yet, even though she confided her anguish to me, she had a great sense of humor and could make me laugh like no one else in the world.

"Eventually, the effect of her constant depressions was to put a wedge between us. It became the worst in my senior year of high school. She would just sit in her room and cry all day. I had two lives: In school I had friends, and at home I had my mother. I didn't know how to talk about it with anyone. I did all the shopping, cooking, and cleaning for both of us.

"My mother would say there's existence and there's life and that she was just existing. She would cry that she was a failure. I would say, 'No, you're not.' Then, she started talking about how it would be better for me if she ended it. I would fly into a rage. 'Don't you ever say that,' I would scream at her. She would back down, explaining that suicide was not in her nature, that she would never do it. But she would say both things—that she would and wouldn't kill herself.

"At the end of my senior year, I went away for the summer to work as a counselor at a summer camp. I was there barely two weeks when I got a call from a neighbor that my mother had been admitted to the psychiatric ward at the hospital. She had been scheduled to go to the hospital for a medical examination but took the subway there wearing her bathrobe and slippers and carrying the dog. They took one look at her and committed her.

"They gave her all these different drugs. Although she was flattened out, she hadn't lost her awareness of what was making her unhappy. When I first came to see her, she rejected me. That had never happened before. I thought she was angry at me because I had gone away for the summer—or tried to—something I had never done before. She was in a trance and a dream state. I started crying to see her like that.

"Eventually, she started coming out of it, and one month later she came home. Soon after, I went away to college, something my mother had encouraged. In my last year of high school, I had focused my whole world around her. Her depression affected me greatly but I couldn't recognize it at the time. I knew that I didn't want to succumb to it. Although she was falling apart, I had to hold myself up. I worked hard and got a full scholarship to a good college around two hours from home.

"When I went away to college, my mother seemed to get better at first. Then, in the spring of my freshman year, she called me to say that she had suffered an extreme anxiety attack walking the dog and had thought she couldn't make it home. She was hyperventilating on the phone. The reality of her situation hit me—she was not going to make it. I realized that she would not be able to survive if she couldn't even walk the dog. I saw very clearly that she would not be able to climb out of the hole, that the walls were closing in.

"There were so many beginning-of-the-ends, but I'm thankful for that day. I knew it was the end. I asked for a leave of absence from school. When I came home, my mother was on a steady plane downward. I found a job near the apartment and one day she called me at work to say that she was thinking of killing herself, that she couldn't hold on anymore. I wanted to jump out of my skin. I felt like I was talking her off the roof, that whatever I said would determine whether she lived or died.

"I told her to hold on, but I felt utterly useless. It seemed as if I were committing suicide with her; I could feel her hopelessness as profoundly as she. Her despair was beyond any talking, any medication, any person, including myself. I had tried to be her cheerleader and support. Yet, I felt my words didn't matter one bit. I started thinking, Why? What were the terms of her life? I bought into her mind-set. Why should she live? Why hold on to life if it is so full of suffering? What's the point—it's all so futile.

"I came home from work. She was just sitting there, like a shell. She didn't want me to leave. Although I convinced her at that moment not to kill herself, I felt at that point my mother had died. For weeks afterward, she would sit in the living room in the dark, wearing only her bathrobe. She was gone, as far as I was concerned. We were like two ships passing in the night. I came to believe that if she wanted to take her life, it was okay—there was nothing left to say.

"I told her I wanted to leave. We had a terrible argument and I exploded in rage. I said that she was manipulating me, that I couldn't take care of her any longer. I told her she had to choose whether to live or to die—it was her life, not mine. She answered, 'You're right,' and we said farewell.

"The next day, I left to stay with my cousin in Houston for a while. It was damned if I did or damned if I didn't. But I knew that if I stayed with my mother, I would die. As I drove to the airport, I realized that I might have seen her for the last time. One week later, I was feeling great. I was living with my cousin and feeling totally liberated and at peace. I spoke to my mother every day. She sounded okay and wasn't talking suicide. Then, my mother's neighbor called to say that she had killed herself. She had jumped out of her seventh-story bedroom window. My first reaction was shock, then relief. Her misery was at an end.

"I flew back to Boston. The only people at her memorial service were me, my father, and the minister. I felt at the time that my mother's pain and sadness were such a secret that I didn't want to have to explain them to others. After my mother's death, I knew I now had to live for myself. I gave up our apartment and sold the furniture. Boston was over. The curtain had dropped and I was starting over.

"I moved to Houston and entered college there. For a couple of years, I was feeling wonderful. I went from a period of tremendous relief to giving birth to myself. Then, about three years after my mother's death, I began to feel a horrible guilt. I started thinking about why I hadn't helped her. Why hadn't I rescued her and found other options to save her? I was flooded with blame. I didn't tell anyone about how I was feeling; I was just being stoic.

"It was as if I had a split personality. The outside of me was going around doing all these things and the inner me was obsessing about why I hadn't saved my mother. I would try to convince myself that there was nothing I could have done, but then I would become consumed again with guilt. Finally, I went for help. I began intensive therapy because I knew I couldn't handle all my problems by myself. I eventually moved back to Boston, where I have devoted myself to my work as a photographer.

"Even though I have come to accept that my mother's life was hers and her death was hers, there's a part of me that still feels guilty for not having found something that would have made her want to live. I have this recurrent dream where my mother is a homeless drug addict writhing in despair. I try to rescue her but I can't. I know that I am a survivor because I just keep plodding on with my life. Although I was not able to save my mother, I didn't want to die along with her. That is a choice I'll have to live with for the rest of my life."

Like Rosemarie, I, too, still have dreams of helplessness and guilt. I am on a wooden platform careening in the noisy sea, frantically stretching out my hand. But Harry does not reach for it. The waves carry me away and he is left alone in the raging storm. I wake up, suffocating from the what-ifs: What if I had moved closer to the edge of the platform? What if I had screamed louder for him to swim over to me? What if I had jumped back in the water and rescued him?

Gradually, I have allowed myself to recognize that it is Harry's preference not to come with me. I can use my hand to wave goodbye but not to pull him alongside me; only he can reach up to me. In order to move on with my life, it is Harry's helplessness, not mine, that I must learn to both acknowledge and accept.

⍥ 8

The Roller Coaster
of Emotions

"Different people suffer pain differently. It is not the degree of the pain but the difference of pain."

—Suicide support group leader

I was not prepared for the violent extremes of emotion that engulfed me after Harry's suicide. In what seemed like seconds, I would careen from feelings of inconsolable sorrow to murderous rage to horrified bewilderment. The reality of what had happened stole my days; relentless nightmares robbed my sleep. I was psychically battered and physically spent.

The rapid changes in mood left me unable to catch my breath. Each time I thought I had discovered the missing piece of the puzzle that would explain Harry's death, my reaction would alter accordingly. Yet, because there was no logical answer to what had been an irrational act, I could find no peace or rest.

"Suicide is the ultimate 'fuck you,' " I would repeat to myself when fury at my husband's abandonment would flood over me. Then, the image of a despondent Harry, facing his death isolated and alone, would fill my thoughts. Physical pains of remorse would overpower me, their intensity causing me to fear that I was dying of heart attack. My anger would be replaced by uncontrollable tears. It was I who had abandoned Harry, I would reproach myself. My body would shake from waves of shame. How could I have been so stupid, I would berate myself. He was planning his suicide and I had not been able to see what was going on. Panic would push away the anguish. This was not real, I would conclude. I must be dreaming or in the middle of a nervous breakdown. I would feel myself physically shrinking, disassociating from the world around me. Then, the reality of Harry's death would jolt me back—and the cacophony of emotions would begin again.

According to Marian Osterweis and Jessica Townsend of the National Institute of Mental Health, sudden death is especially shocking for those who are left behind because it precludes the possibility of preparation. They point out that 80 percent of all deaths in the United States occur with several weeks' warning, adding: "More psychological distress is experienced by family members following death by suicide than death by natural causes. Heightened anger directed at the deceased and guilt for not having been able to prevent the death, as well as true clinical depression, are more likely to occur and persist."

The authors conclude that whether or not a death is anticipated, the bereavement process following the loss of a loved one takes several years. They observe that for many people, the second year is more difficult than the first. In addition, the mourning process does not necessarily progress in an orderly fashion. People move back and forth between what the authors describe as overlapping and fluid stages, and act in ways that might be considered abnormal under other circumstances. People differ in how rapidly they recover and how they express their grief after a death. The most immediate response, however, is shock, numbness, and a sense of disbelief. There are dramatic and rapid swings from one state to another, including depressed moods, difficulty in concentrating, anger at the deceased for dying, guilt about what might have been done to avoid the death, irritability, anxiety, restlessness, and extreme sadness. People also experience numerous physical symptoms, such as pain, gastrointestinal upset, lack of energy and sleep, and appetite disturbances.

The distinctive bereavement process following a suicide is described in an *American Journal of Psychiatry* article, written by Drs. David Ness and Cynthia Pfeffer, which concludes that family members who have lost a loved one to suicide are blamed and avoided more often than relatives of people who have died under other circumstances. The article points out that this attitude may reinforce the guilt and self-blame that already preoccupy suicide survivors, exacerbating their isolation and difficulty in talking about their feelings.

As survivors move from absorbing the impact of the suicide to dealing with the consequences of the loss, we begin to embark on our own individual journey of healing. Yet, in the process of moving on, we also experience tremendous guilt that our lives have not stopped with the death of our loved one.

I remember the feeling of alarm that came over me the first time I was able to become absorbed with something unrelated to Harry's suicide. It was several months after he had killed himself. My days were totally consumed with the practical logistics of putting my life back into order; my nights were filled with the unrelenting emotional fallout that prevented me from sleeping. I envied people who had the luxury to concern themselves with such minor annoyances as the dry cleaners ruining their clothes or their bus being delayed in traffic; I longed for the boring and routine.

I was at the dentist's office to replace a filling that had fallen out the day before. Even the act of making the appointment seemed like a betrayal of Harry's memory: How could I engage in such a mundane activity at the same time I was struggling to resolve the ultimate philosophical question of what makes some people want to live and others choose to die? The care of my tooth seemed absolutely inconsequential—almost laughable—compared with the anguish that Harry must have been suffering. Yet, here I was, selfishly taking care of my insignificant needs.

I had come to believe that my ability to concentrate had been permanently impaired by Harry's suicide. I was not able to read, watch television, engage in a conversation for more than a few minutes before the recollection of the events surrounding his death would ambush my thoughts. I considered myself disabled, a casualty of a vicious war.

There was a copy of *People* magazine in the dentist's waiting room. I started thumbing through it, when an article recounting the latest scandals of a notorious actor caught my attention. I read for what seemed like several minutes before I heard my name being called by the receptionist. I was startled to discover that I had become so engaged in this man's marital and drug problems that I had forgotten about myself. I was suddenly infused with hope for my future: For the first time since the suicide, I had been able to concentrate completely without images of Harry interrupting my attention. Even though my optimism was almost simultaneously replaced by profound guilt—I was forsaking my husband's memory—I knew on some gut level that I had not been left irreparably damaged, that I was on my way to becoming whole again.

Many survivors discover strengths and inner resources they never knew existed following the suicide of a loved one. "In one second, I went from being a child to being a man," recalls Lewis, a forty-one-year-old hospital administrator from Tulsa whose father killed himself one week before Lewis graduated from high school. "He always overprotected me, and his death was my first lesson in the 'real' problems of the 'real' world. As the oldest son, I was left to take care of my mother and younger brothers. Because of my father's suicide, I lost out on an important part of my growing up. Instead of going to college, I stayed home and took a job. I felt forced to assume my father's role as provider for the family. It took me a while to be able to express my anger at what he had done. Although I felt guilty that I was being disloyal to his memory, it was the only way I could begin to start my own life.

"I don't remember my father ever being depressed until the last couple of months of my senior year in high school. I had received a baseball scholarship at a small college around two hours from my home, and my father kept on saying that this would be the last summer the whole family would be together. He was really upset about this. I would assure him that I would come home for vacations, but he would always answer me with the same comment: 'It's the end of an era.' I was so involved with my own problems—teenage stuff, like who to invite to the prom—that I didn't see what was going on with him.

"The Saturday before my graduation was my team's big game. My father always came to see me play; he would even

come to practice. We were alone in the house and I was waiting for him to drive me over to school. All of a sudden, I heard
a loud bang in the backyard. My next-door neighbor was
screaming and I ran outside. My father had shot himself in the
head. For some reason, I was very calm. I walked back into the
house in what seemed slow motion and called the police. I was
in the kitchen and I remember seeing my father's half-eaten
toast and the paper opened to the sports pages. His coffee was
still warm. I went back out to my father and cradled him in my
arms. I knew he was dead but I kept on talking to him. I
remember all this yelling and commotion around me. I was
covered with his blood but it didn't seem to matter. I knew
beyond a doubt that he had killed himself because I was going
to leave him. In my mind, I just accepted total responsibility
for his death.

"Although I had really loved my father, for some reason I
was unable to cry when he died. I became the man of the
house and took over the responsibilities of looking after my
family. Around six months after my father died, my best friend
came home from college for Christmas vacation. He was going on and on about school and sports and girls. It all seemed
so far away from me. For the first time, I became mad at my
father for leaving me with all his shit. But then I quickly erased
that thought from my mind, as if I were being a bad son.

"As the months went on, I started feeling as if I were
drowning. One day, my mother said to me that she was worried I was becoming like my father. I had no idea what she
meant. She reluctantly told me that my father had suffered
from depression when he was younger and had been hospitalized for a suicide attempt when I was two years old. I was
crushed—how could she have kept that information from me?

"It was only after his death that I began learning about my
father's life. It was like working backward. The more I knew,

the angrier I became. Why should I have to give up my life because he was sick? I started having terrible nightmares. I was always screaming at a man who was trying to run away from me. I was terrified that I would end up crazy like my father. I was convinced that I was losing it and knew I needed help.

"My priest suggested that I attend a support group for suicide survivors that met in a nearby town. Walking into that meeting was very difficult for me. But it was the beginning of my healing. I was able to rant and rave against my father with people who did not judge me for being selfish or cruel. I even felt safe enough to cry. The more I allowed myself to see my father's suicide as his choice, the more I knew I had to get on with what I wanted to do. My mother was financially stable, my brothers were doing well in school, and I was ready to take my life back.

"Now, I am regarded as very successful in my community. I am engaged to a wonderful woman, have a responsible job, and coach the local Little League team. I guess you can say that I have moved on from the devastation of my father's suicide. Yet, especially when I'm feeling good, I start thinking that I really could have done more for my father. I kick myself for being a self-centered teenager who should have spent more time with him. I also feel deceived that I didn't know about his previous attempt to kill himself when I was growing up. I'm convinced that it would have made a difference in how I acted toward him. Twenty-three years after his death, it seems as if I still have the same set of emotions. The difference is that they are not as intense and don't swing back and forth with the same frequency. I have these relatively long periods of calm, which allow me to function and even thrive."

The irrationality of suicide leaves the survivor no room for definitive resolution. "In order for me to move beyond my partner's suicide, I need to accept it as a purely existential act," explains Lena, a thirty-four-year-old actress from New York City. "Charles and I had been in a loving, committed relationship for three years. He was a sculptor whose work was just beginning to become recognized. I search myself and search myself but I cannot recall any signs that Charles was even vaguely unhappy. We talked about just everything, so I thought I really knew him. God knows, I was wrong.

"It was one of those lazy Sunday mornings, last August. I went down to the basement to do the laundry. When I came back up to the apartment, I heard all this commotion on the street. The window was wide open and there was this beautiful photograph that Charles had taken of me taped to the sill. He had written "I love you" across the bottom. I knew then that he had jumped. I started screaming and could hear my voice echoing, as if it didn't belong to me. I remember ripping the picture to shreds and throwing it out the window after him.

"Charles's suicide left me furious. We didn't get a chance to say goodbye. For weeks, I was in total raw shock, as if I had been in a fire and all my skin was burned off. Luckily, I was already in therapy and had a very supportive network of close friends. Gradually, my anger abated and I was able to begin mourning him. Yet, every time I seemed to start feeling better, this automatic reflex would kick in and I would begin to assault myself for being so blind and self-involved that I neglected to see what must have been going on with him. I would blame myself for having left him alone so I could go do the laundry, of all things.

"Lately, I've been trying to go out more and not be so solitary. Yet, when I find myself starting to have a good time or wanting to begin dating again, I feel unfaithful to Charles. I'm trying to incorporate his suicide into my life, to find a balance between remembering him and establishing a new life for myself. It is probably the hardest thing I've ever had to do."

The roller coaster of emotions following a suicide causes intense feelings of isolation and a breaking apart from all that once seemed familiar. "Six months ago, we had a round of layoffs at work and two of my colleagues committed suicide shortly afterward," says Brenda, a fifty-eight-year-old secretary at a large law firm in Chicago. "My husband and children tell me that something is wrong with me because I'm taking their deaths so hard. It's true that they were not my closest friends, but I feel so guilty because I still have my job while they lost theirs. Why is that so? I keep wondering what would have happened if they hadn't been laid off. Would they still have killed themselves?

"There was a group of us who worked on the same shift for four years. Our desks were right near each other. We would go out to lunch together and occasionally see each other socially. Mostly, though, we shared our problems with each other—both personal and work-related. One Friday afternoon, two-thirds of the office staff were fired, with no warning from management. It wasn't based on seniority and we were all shocked. I felt very disoriented, even though for some reason I had kept my job.

"Three months after she was fired from her secretarial job, Maria, a thirty-one-year-old single mother of a four-year-old boy, slit her wrists. She was on life support at the hospital for two days before she finally died. When her mother called to tell me what had happened, I was shocked. I had always thought of Maria as unbelievably strong. It was also my first experience with suicide. My first reaction was terrible sadness for the loss of such a young person. Then I became angry. How could she have left her son, who needed her? Why had she been so weak to have given up when she had so much to live for? To leave everything behind because you lose a job? I couldn't believe it.

"Her wake was awful. They had an open casket, but it didn't look like her. The expression on her face was troubled, almost angry. There was an extremely emotional reaction from her coworkers. We were like a family with a very close bond. Then, one month after her funeral, Faye, a paralegal who also had been fired, killed herself by taking an overdose of sleeping pills. She was twenty-six years old and had been in and out of hospitals since she was a teenager because of anorexia. She was always talking about death, how dead people are luckier than us. We would tell her she was beautiful, that she had so much to live for. But it didn't seem to make an impact.

"Faye's condition became much worse after she was laid off. She was down to fifty-four pounds, and in the hospital when Maria killed herself. We debated whether or not to tell her because she had looked up to Maria as very strong and a real fighter. We decided she had the right to know, but now I think we made a mistake. At the wake, Faye just stared at Maria's body and looked desperate. Afterward, she went to visit her mother in Pennsylvania for a couple of weeks.

"She had been back in Chicago for one week when her psychiatrist called her mother to say that she hadn't shown up for her appointment. One of the conditions of Faye's release from the hospital was that she had to see him or she would have to be readmitted. Her mother called the police. They went to Faye's apartment and found her body. She had left notes for different people and had prepared bags filled with carefully selected items for each one of her friends.

"My first reaction was, thank God, Faye's torment is finally over. She suffered so long and has now found peace. I told myself she had finally done what she had wanted to do for so long. I feel bad that this was my reaction, but it's the truth. We had tried to get her help all the time but nothing had worked.

"I feel so different about the deaths of these two young women. I think that Faye is at peace but I'm angry at Maria. Yet, everyone who is left behind is devastated, no matter what. We all have big-time guilt that we could have done more. There was no sense of closure at either funeral, just a feeling that neither one of them really cared about the rest of us. Even though they were in different states of mind, I really believe that suicide is an extremely selfish act. I try to think of Maria and Faye as mentally ill but it doesn't help.

"Now, the mood at the office is much more somber. Those of us who are left don't hang out together anymore and we've stopped talking about Maria and Faye. The human resources department at work didn't offer us any kind of counseling; no representative from management came to either funeral. Just yesterday, I told the office manager that I had to take one day off next week. She said sarcastically, 'Not another funeral, I hope.'

"I'm thinking about looking for another job. This is a cold place and feels cursed. I've also begun to realize how short life is. I don't want to die, and I pray that I never get into that state where I might even consider killing myself. I accept that suicide is a way out but I don't want to do it. Recently, though, I find myself reading into what people are saying, thinking they might be giving off signals that they are considering killing themselves. I lost my father, but my reaction to his death was very different—I viewed it as following the natural course of God's plans. I'm now filled with feelings of mortality; like it or not, suicide has become a part of my life."

Some survivors are able to accept the idea of suicide more easily than others, resigning themselves to its power and permanency. "I feel completely comfortable with my brother's decision to kill himself," says Martin, a forty-nine-year-old architect from Miami. "I'm not sure that his reasons for ending his life shouldn't remain mysterious. I didn't kill myself. I was minding my own business—it was his choice."

Martin's brother committed suicide twenty years ago, when he was a first-year medical student. "I was on my honeymoon when my parents called me to say that Jimmy had shot himself. My life changed from that minute on. I believe that there are external lives and internal lives, and the two of mine became completely separate at Jimmy's suicide. My parents were devastated. Jimmy was always the golden boy in my family, the brilliant son who was going to win a Nobel prize. I was the screwed-up one, the artist. If one of us was more likely to kill himself, it seemed that it should have been me.

"I've become very fatalistic since my brother died. My philosophy is something along the line of, 'If you're not hung, you're shot.' I find myself taking chances all the time. I love flying my plane, especially into a storm. I make a lot of money, then lose it, then make some more. Everything is pretty transitory. In a way, I consider Jimmy to be very courageous. He faced death eye to eye—he controlled his destiny, not the other way around. I admire him for that."

Even though survivors experience a wide range of often contradictory emotions following the suicide of a loved one, its impact alters our lives forever. Shortly after Harry's death, I began to despair of ever being able to come to terms with his choice to die, to leave me so alone. Although I was talking about his suicide with my therapist, selected friends, and the members of my support group, I was growing more and more discouraged. All this rehashing and reconstructing was getting me nowhere, I would tell myself.

One evening, I dragged myself to a support meeting, vowing it would be the last one I attended. That night, a woman told the story of her son's suicide, which had occurred more than thirty-five years earlier. Sophie was in her late seventies, a retired opera singer who had performed with leading houses all over the world. When her son was fourteen, she returned home to find him hanging from a light fixture in his bedroom. As treatment for her ensuing depression, her doctor ordered shock therapy to try to erase the incident from her consciousness. It seemed to work, and Sophie was left with only blurry impressions of the events surrounding her son's death.

About two years ago, Sophie told the mesmerized group, she had become filled with detailed memories of her son's suicide, specific recollections she thought had been obliterated in the past thirty years. Since then, she went on, she had started reliving the suicide almost obsessively and had begun suffering recurrent nightmares filled with terrifying images of her dead son.

"You can never escape," she said. "I don't know what triggered me, but I am now consumed by my son's suicide. Over these past many years, his death had seemed to be theater, something I had seen on stage. I was completely detached from what had happened. I was not prepared for my past to just descend on me. Now, I'm beginning to accept that you can't hide from what happens to you. You have to go through it to get through it."

That night, I cried for Sophie and her poor, young son. I cried for all the people at the meetings who had lost someone so dear to them in a manner so inexplicable and wrenching. I cried for Harry, dead in his prime, preempting the ending to his life without waiting to see what might have laid ahead. But I knew that I had to listen to Sophie's advice in order to heal. I had to endure the hollowness, the guilt, the anguish, the anger, in order to emerge on the other side. There is no easy way to eradicate the pain of grieving. I would have to try to keep my balance until the roller coaster of emotions finished its course. Then, I could get off, walk on my own, and truly move on with my life.

Legal and
Financial Problems

> *"Homeowners, beware. That gorgeous house you're*
> *about to buy may have been the scene of a gory*
> *murder, suicide or some other stigma."*
>
> —New York *Daily News*, August 11, 1995

The local media heralded the news that in 1995 New York State had joined with more than half the states in the country in passing a law exempting real estate agents and owners from disclosing the histories of the homes they sell or the apartments they rent. I had finally sold Harry's medical office after a torturous ordeal that involved struggling with reluctant agents, an antagonistic condominium board, obstructive neighbors, and superstitious buyers. The new ruling, therefore, was too late to offer me much relief. Instead, I focused on the story of the woman featured in a *New York Times* article who, while trying to sell her property, had been forced to tell and retell prospective buyers the details of her husband's shooting himself on the deck of their house.

"People have a phobia about suicide," she explained. "As soon as I disclosed that my husband had killed himself, they didn't want to buy." Eventually, she took the house off the market in order to avoid having to repeat the painful story of her husband's death. "What happens inside or outside the home has absolutely no bearing at all," she said. "When it comes to suicide, it is a very personal matter. This is very difficult for me."

As much as I tried to protect myself from talking about the true circumstances of Harry's death, the reality was that his suicide could not have been more public. My husband's office was located in a twelve-story condominium in downtown Manhattan. Within minutes of the discovery of his body, the entire area had been turned into an instant crime scene. Police officers, the ambulance crew, members of the medical examiner's office swarmed throughout the building. Detectives interviewed me in the lobby, with curious spectators taking in every word. Police from the local precinct questioned apartment residents and members of the staff in order to rule out homicide as a possible cause of death.

Two years later, after three potential sales of the office had fallen through, my financial situation was bordering on desperate. Harry and I had taken out a second mortgage on our home in order to purchase his medical practice. The monthly carrying charges of the condominium were extremely high, and I still owed thousands of dollars in outstanding construction loans. Harry's empty office—the site of his self-executed death—was draining not only my emotional strength but also my monetary resources.

When the first two purchasers backed off after expressing great interest in the property, I half-seriously began to blame Harry's ghost for obstructing the sale. "I'm afraid that he is pulling me down with him," I confided to my therapist. Logically, I knew I was speaking from the unresolved guilt that was coloring every part of my life. Yet, when a friend suggested that I burn sage to rid the office of any remaining spirits, I followed her advice. Something was spooking away the buyers.

The third deal fell apart a week before closing. I had to face the fact that whatever was going on was not a result of supernatural causes or mere coincidence. I confronted the once-enthusiastic purchaser, an internist who was just beginning his private practice. Embarrassed, he explained that he had been approached by the owner of a medical office in the building who had advised him not to buy, recounting Harry's suicide in lurid detail. Although the young doctor expressed sympathy for my loss, he did not feel that seeing patients in Harry's office would be a particularly auspicious beginning for his medical career.

It seemed that whatever little strength I had left evaporated at that minute. Like the woman quoted in the article, I felt as if the negative fallout from Harry's suicide would never go away. Although I eventually was able to sell the office at a public auction, the consequences of my husband's decision to kill himself continued to reverberate for years after his death.

"Stigma" is the real estate industry's terminology for a property where a murder or suicide has occurred. This type of characterization serves to reinforce the shame and intensify the confusion of emotions experienced by the survivor after a suicide. We soon discover that the concept of stigma is not only a psychological burden but also a legal and financial problem that affects our ability to heal and move on with our lives.

"I was totally unprepared for what happened in the aftermath of my father's suicide," says Elizabeth, a fifty-seven-year-old nurse from New Jersey. "Six years ago, my father shot himself two hours before Thanksgiving dinner. My family had come to my parents' house in Iowa from all across the country. Instead of celebrating, we spent the day cleaning up my father's blood."

Elizabeth stayed in Iowa for several weeks to help her mother put her legal and financial affairs in order. "Suicide wreaks such devastating havoc," she states. "Immediately after my father killed himself, the police questioned each member of the family, one by one, treating us as if we were suspects in a murder-conspiracy plot. We all sat around the kitchen feeling like criminals while they searched the house. I still have no idea what they were looking for. We had the bad luck of having an officer who believed in doing the entire investigation by the book. I felt insane, like I was part of a dark comedy or a Kafka novel. Here was my father's body lying in the dining room until the medical examiner could arrive to pronounce him dead, the police hunting for some sort of 'evidence,' and my family staring at each other in total shock and disbelief.

"The next day, my brother and I had to go to court to prove that my mother, he, and I were the only heirs to the estate. Unbelievably, my father had died without a will. This was the first sign of what lay ahead as we began to discover the total disarray in which he had left his business. In order to have the body released, we had to prove that we could pay for the funeral. All day we had to deal with bureaucratic hassle. It was like trying to get your passport or driver's license and just added to the surrealness of the situation.

"I spoke with the minister about plans for the funeral. He explained that while there was no official church position on suicide, he, personally, would not be comfortable conducting the services at my father's funeral. He added that it would be possible, however, for my father to be buried in the main section of the cemetery. I was stunned. Maybe I was naive, but I never even considered that there would be any question about the religious arrangements. Everything I was doing was related to my father's *suicide;* the fact that he had *died* seemed to be lost along the way.

"After the funeral, I hired a lawyer to expedite the process of naming my mother executor of my father's estate. Until the decree was granted, their joint savings account was frozen. My brother and I had to support her during this time. As I sat in my childhood home trying to make sense of all the bills, I found my shock and sorrow turning to resentment. It wasn't as if my father had been hit by a car and had no time to get his life in order. Yet, I also understood that his manner of death reflected the disorganization and loss of control he must have been feeling while he was planning to blow his brains out. But why do something so extreme, so devastating to my mother?

"The only bright spot was that my father had a life insurance policy he had bought years before that ended up saving my mother from being forced to declare bankruptcy. Yet, even as a tenuous kind of order returned to my mother's life, she became more isolated from her friends and even stopped her volunteer work at the church. I know she was deeply ashamed about what my father had done, but she wouldn't talk about it to anyone. One year after my father died, she discovered a lump in her breast. By the time she finally went to the doctor, the cancer had already metastasized to her lungs. She had no interest in fighting the disease and died within months. On a certain level, I blame my father for her death. The toll that suicide exacts on its survivors is very high, unfortunately."

Most survivors are unprepared for the practical concerns that follow a suicide. It is impossible to imagine that the police will question us about the circumstances surrounding our father's death or that the minister will place conditions on our daughter's funeral or that the court will question the legitimacy of our husband's will. In addition, the psychological implication of classifying suicide a crime complicates our response to the death of our loved one.

"My sister was killed one year ago when she slammed into a dividing wall on the highway," says Brian, a thirty-one-year-old editor from Lansing, Michigan. "The police initially investigated the case as a potential suicide. My mother was virtually destroyed by the constant probing into my sister's private life. Yet, even though her death was eventually ruled accidental, in all honesty there's a part of me that believes my sister intentionally drove her car into that wall. Ten years before, our father died in a small-plane crash. My sister was always convinced that he flew into the woods near the airport on purpose in order for my mother to collect his insurance money. We were having a lot of financial problems at the time and my sister believed my father's committing suicide was his way of salvaging the situation for the family. I used to think she was crazy, but now I don't know. About her or about him."

According to the book *McGill's Life Insurance*, some of the early court decisions in the United States found that death by suicide should not be covered by a life insurance policy. "Suicide is contrary to many religious laws," the book states, "and attempted suicide is ordinarily a penal offense. Thus suicide is contrary to public policy." Although this view was later rejected in the United States, denial of life insurance as the result of suicide is still the law in England. Presently, most life insurance companies in the United States are not liable for policies taken out within two years of a suicide.

"Money should have been the least of my problems, but the anxiety of not knowing how I was going to support myself and my unborn child only increased my despair," says Carol, a forty-year-old magazine publisher from Minneapolis whose husband drowned himself four years ago, when she was nine months pregnant. "I had no idea if the insurance company would pay me after Josh's death. I just assumed that when you kill yourself, forget it. Anyway, who even thinks of a suicide clause when you buy life insurance? Even with the money from Josh's policy, financially I still got creamed. We had used up all our savings to buy a big old house, our 'dream house.' I ended up selling it at a total loss.

"Suicide is like a public divorce and a homicide at the same time. It was incredible that in the middle of trying to absorb the shock of Josh's suicide, I was having to deal with creditors, banks, insurance companies, and an endless number of lawyers. It was really quite humbling—a new house, a baby on the way. I was on top of the world. Josh's suicide certainly showed me how fragile life can be. You think everything is wonderful and then your world blows up.

"Josh was fired from his job as an assistant district attorney on a Friday afternoon of a long holiday weekend. He never told me about it; he never even let on that he was having problems at work. Over the weekend, he was frantically trying to get the house in order even though we had just moved in. He was unpacking boxes and putting things away. I remember asking him what the rush was, reminding him—and this is very painful—that we had all the time in the world to create the perfect home for our new baby.

"On Tuesday morning, I left for work before Josh, which

was very unusual. I even said to him, 'This is a first.' He was taking out the garbage and blew me some kisses. My husband was a meticulous dresser but I noticed that his shirt collar was frayed. It passed through my mind that this was also out of character for him, but I forced myself to dismiss my instinct that something might be wrong.

"I was on deadline and was not able to call Josh until around four in the afternoon. His secretary sounded surprised and told me that he no longer worked there. I was floored. I demanded that she put my husband's boss on the phone. He got on the line and told me that Josh had been terminated, that his employment there had not been a good fit. As soon as I heard that, I knew in my heart that Josh had killed himself. He had wanted this job very badly and it was very important to him. I called home but no one answered. Now I had no doubt that Josh was dead.

"I felt very alone. My parents were in Europe and my sister was trekking in Nepal. I tried convincing myself that I was this hysterical pregnant woman, that Josh might become depressed about being fired but he would never commit suicide over it. Instead of going home, I drove to our old apartment in the city, which we were still trying to sell. It was my fantasy, even though I really never believed it, that I would find him sitting in the dark, waiting for me to come get him. He wasn't there, of course.

"I was afraid to go back to our house by myself. Maybe I thought I would find him dead in there. I drove to his aunt's house in a nearby suburb. She was eighty years old and I always believed in her wisdom. She told me that Josh was probably driving around, getting his thoughts together. I kept on calling the house but the machine kept picking up. By midnight his aunt also became worried. It had started raining hard, so we began calling up the area hospitals to see if he had been in an accident. We were up all night. In the morning, I called Josh's brother in California. He said Josh was probably just off somewhere, cooling his jets. Yet, I knew something was wrong. Josh was always very considerate. He would never make me worry unless something was desperately wrong.

"I finally called a close friend, who left work and came right over. She called the police, who told her I should check the house before filing a missing persons report. My friend told me she would drive over to the house with me and we could walk in together. I don't know what I expected to find, but everything there seemed so normal, so untouched. It was as if Josh had disappeared without a trace.

"I was numbed out—nothing seemed as if it was really happening to me. My friend and I then went to the police station. Although I was treated with respect, I could see that ·the police were skeptical when I told them about my fears that Josh had committed suicide. They were very polite but just kept on asking all these police-type questions, like if Josh had another woman or if he had been depressed. Even though they put out an all-points bulletin, they advised me to hire a criminal investigator to help with the search. They also recommended that I call everyone in his telephone book and check the hotels in all the cities and places he loved.

"My friend wanted me to move in with her, pleading with me to think of the baby. But I felt safer staying with Josh's aunt. The next day, I had my childbirth class. On the way over, my friend confided that she had a gut feeling Josh would be waiting for me there. But I knew he was dead; I had no hope. After class, I called his father. He told me that the pressure of Josh's being fired could have put him over the edge. Then I called his sister, who is married to a psychiatrist. She and her husband both thought I might be right, he could have possibly killed himself. For the first time since Josh disappeared, I felt validated.

"My parents came home from Europe two days later. When I saw them, I collapsed in tears. I moved in with them right away. From that moment on, they didn't leave me alone. I think they were afraid I would kill myself. Yet, as much as I wanted to die, I knew I wanted to live. I was not going to make two tragedies out of this.

"I went back to work. I forced myself to go to the ballet, to get a manicure, to restructure some kind of normal life. I would not let myself fall apart. One of my friends advised me to leave a message on my home answering machine for Josh, asking him to come home, that all was forgiven. I said, No, I'm still on the map. He knew how to find me. Besides, it was Josh who was missing, not me.

"The next Sunday, almost two weeks after Josh had left, the police came to my parents' house. Boaters had discovered Josh's body in a lake around five hours from where we lived. He was wearing weights on his ankles and wrists, and his knapsack was filled with barbells. I was at a friend's house when my parents called to tell me. My mother said, 'Really bad news, Carol.' I answered, 'How did he kill himself?' It was as if I had known all along.

"Josh's car was found on a deserted road near the lake. Inside was a suicide note dated the day he disappeared. The police gave me a photocopy because they have to keep the original on file. Josh had addressed the note to me. 'I really fucked up,' he wrote. 'We should not have bought the house. Was the baby a boy or a girl?' He also mentioned his insurance policy, how he hoped I would find another man, and that he loved me very much. The note was three pages long.

"Two weeks after they recovered Josh's body, my daughter

was born. Childbirth was anguishing, both physically and emotionally. I saw all these other husbands with their wives. I missed out on the bliss. I missed out on the tenderness of having a husband to give me a back rub or kiss my forehead as I was giving birth to our baby. Here I was with my mother instead of my husband. For the first time, I let myself be angry at Josh and everyone else around me.

"My numbness cracked after the birth of my daughter. Josh's death finally became real and I felt very much alone. My first reaction was terrible fear—I did not see how I would be able to make it work. My parents kept saying they would help me out, but I knew that if I continued living with them I would feel like I was a sixteen-year-old kid with an illegitimate baby. I wanted to establish an independent life for my daughter and me. Three months later, I moved into my own apartment and went back to work.

"It has taken me a long time to straighten out the practical details of my life. In a way, conducting such mundane and ordinary business matters as selling my house, settling my banking matters, and finding child care for my daughter protected me from having to think about what Josh had done. As the dust begins to settle, his suicide is starting to seem less black-and-white and more gray. I find myself trying to incorporate many of his good qualities, like his patience and caring, into my relationship with my daughter. What I can never forgive him for, however, is the legacy of abandonment he has left behind. My daughter will have to live with his rejection for the rest of her life. Suicide is such a mess. It is unbelievable how one person's decision can affect so many lives."

Like Carol, survivors must use every ounce of strength to fight against being swept away by the swirling chaos that suicide leaves in its wake. As we try to assimilate the shock of losing a person we love in such a violent and bruising manner, we crave for the return of what used to be our normal routine. Putting our legal and financial affairs in order is often the first step toward restoring a sense of wholeness to our shattered lives.

The night before I finally closed on the sale of Harry's office, I stood alone in the empty darkness at the exact spot where he had killed himself. "I am letting this go, Harry," I spoke out loud. "You will always be in my heart. But I have to move on. I don't need turmoil not to forget you. I want to start remembering the good parts—and there were many, many good parts."

The sale went through, allowing me to pay my bills, including the long overdue accounts extended to me by my compassionate lawyers, accountant, and therapist. Clearing my debts, relinquishing my responsibility for Harry's office, closing the books on my legal fees and consultations was the beginning of my moving on. I was tidying up the remains of what Harry had left behind and looking forward to living, once again, in the present tense.

Part Four

THE SURVIVAL

Beginning
the Mourning

*"A suicidal person is like a black hole of pain. You can
give and give but you just can't fill it up."*

—Suicide support group leader

My father died when I was twenty-nine years old. It was
my first experience with losing someone close to me,
someone I loved very much. I had always dreaded his dying.
He was the anchor in my life, my protector and ardent sup-
porter. I was afraid that I would not be able to survive his loss,
that I would somehow fall apart when he was no longer here.

My father's death was swift and dignified. A respected
author and educator, he was a Pulitzer prize–winning journal-

ist who had been education editor of *The New York Times* for twenty-three years. He was lecturing in Korea as the guest of the government when he suddenly suffered a fatal heart attack. He died, as he wanted, with his boots on, at the age of seventy-two.

My grief was immense. To my surprise, however, I did not break or even splinter. I mourned, I cried, I felt the first stirring of my own mortality. But I remained whole, a testament, I believed, to my father's legacy that life should be embraced, not merely endured.

Six months after my father's death, I began to experience excruciating pains in my chest. At first, I just assumed I was having sympathetic heart attack symptoms and dismissed any physical basis for my growing discomfort. Even as the episodes became more frequent and severe, I refused to go for medical attention. I was convinced that my problem was psychosomatic, a manifestation of the terrible grief I was feeling about my father's death.

One day, as I lay writhing on my living room floor, it passed through my mind that if I jumped out the window, my unbearable suffering would stop. I did not want to die, that I knew, I just wanted to put an end to the pain. The solution seemed so easy, so logical. I would do anything not to feel this way.

Needless to say, I did not go crashing through the window. Instead, trembling with fear, I took a taxi to the emergency room of the hospital where Harry was doing his internship. After a battery of tests, I was informed that my gallbladder was inflamed and I needed immediate surgery. The cause of my problem was neither dramatic nor romantic, just ordinary, mundane, pedestrian gallstones.

Memories of that last, terrible attack descended on me from out of nowhere as the second anniversary of Harry's

suicide approached. I found myself reliving not only the suffo-
cation of my crushing pain but also the feeling of violent
urgency to do anything to stop it. Is this how Harry felt, I
wondered. Was his pain, his psychic pain, so intractable that
only self-murder could end it? Was it possible he really did
not want to die but truly believed he had run out of options to
extinguish his torment?

Primo Levi, the noted author and scholar who survived
the horrors of the Holocaust, only to kill himself forty years
later, wrote in his last book, *The Drowned and the Saved:* "Suicide
is the act of man and not of the animal. It is a meditated act, a
noninstinctive, unnatural choice." Because my father's death
was part of a natural continuum, I was able to mourn his loss
by celebrating his life. Harry's determination to die, however,
offered me no such spiritual balm. Like most survivors, I was
consumed with finding the reason for my husband's "unnatural
choice" to kill himself. Gradually, I came to accept that I
would never understand his motive to cease living; there was
no rational explanation for his irreversible act.

The term *rational suicide* is an oxymoron. When a person
chooses to die, he or she is so distorted by pain—physical,
mental, or emotional—that the world is reduced to a solitary
alternative. Suicide is an anguished response to loss: the loss
of faith, of a loved one, of health, of mental powers, of
money, of the ability to fight. As we survivors separate ourselves from the hopelessness and desperation that propelled
our loved ones to end their lives, we start to mourn their
deaths, not their suicides, and begin to heal from the very real
pain deep within us.

"My brother's death left me as a poet without words," says
Rachel, a fifty-five-year-old New Yorker whose work has been
published in leading literary journals throughout the country.
"I was stunned when Paul shot himself. I kept wanting to be

able to write about what had happened, but I had lost the capacity to express myself. I was afraid that my gift had been extinguished by his suicide, that I would never get my art back again. At the beginning, I couldn't concentrate long enough to read a magazine or watch the news on television, let alone create my poetry.

"Paul was a brilliant scientist, a fierce achiever who received his doctorate in physics at MIT when he was only twenty-seven years old. After he graduated, he was asked to teach at a prestigious Ivy League university. He married his high school sweetheart and was working on an international research project. Then, suddenly, his personality began to change. He became paranoid and delusional; he was acting crazy, to be precise. My parents and his wife took him to a series of doctors. They eventually diagnosed his condition as the sudden onset of manic depression, which hits some men in their late twenties, early thirties.

"The doctors placed Paul on different types of medication but nothing seemed to work. They even put him in a mental institution for thirty days. The day he was released from the hospital, he bought a gun and drove to a park near his house and shot himself in the heart. It was two weeks before his twenty-ninth birthday.

"I believe that Paul killed himself because he knew his condition would only deteriorate, and he did not want to live like that. I'm also convinced that even if he was aware of the devastating consequences his act would have on the rest of us, he still would have gone through with it. Suicide is very selfish. With the force of one bullet, Paul blew away all the history we shared together. Suddenly, I was alone with my parents, the sole guardian of my childhood memories.

"I was thirty-six when Paul died. I had just published my first book of poetry and had won a grant to start on my next collection. It took me more than two years to be able to write again. I knew I had to start with his suicide, but it was as if my putting words to such a dark and frightening act would give it an undeserved validity. Although I used my isolation as protection, I was also silenced by it. When my voice gradually returned, I was overjoyed. Over these past years, my poetry has helped me to relinquish my pain and, in some small way, to keep Paul alive."

As suicide survivors begin the long, arduous process of navigating the labyrinth of our loss, we face the risk of confronting a reality that is often covert and always ambiguous. "Catharsis is important not only to purge but also to clarify," states Larry Lockridge, a literature professor and the son of Ross Lockridge, Jr., the author of *Raintree County*. He was five years old when his father poisoned himself with carbon monoxide fumes from his car exhaust, and eleven before he learned the truth about his father's death. "Clarification is the first, necessary step in a survivor's journey of healing," he says.

Patricia, a junior at the University of Vermont, was twelve years old when she came home from school one day to find her mother dead in the kitchen. "The oven was turned on and there was gas all over the place," she recalls. "I ran screaming over to a neighbor's house, as if I were in one of those horror movies you always see. My mother had been very depressed since my brother was killed in an accident in the army the year before. Many times, I would come from school to find her crying. When I tried to comfort her, she would tell me that I shouldn't worry about grown-up problems, that I should enjoy being young. My mother's suicide created a scandal in our small town. My father refused to discuss it with me and my two sisters, and we lived our whole childhood without even mentioning my mother's name, in *any* context.

"I grew up believing that ending your life makes a lot of

sense if things get too bad. I would wonder why anyone would even want to stay alive if they were really miserable. As soon as I went off to college, my father remarried. At his wedding, one of my cousins told me he was happy for my father, especially after everything he had been through. I took a deep breath and asked, 'You mean my mother?' He answered, 'Yes, and your brother.'

"I felt my stomach go rigid. 'What happened to my brother?' I demanded to know. My cousin was very embarrassed. 'He shot himself the day before his unit was supposed to go overseas,' he replied. 'I thought you knew that.' I walked away in a daze to look for my father. In the middle of the celebration, I confronted him about my brother. He just said calmly, yes, it was true that my brother had died by his own hand—my father would never use the word *suicide*—but that he didn't want to talk about it.

"When I went back to school, I started having terrible stomach problems. The doctors from the health service gave me all these tests but they couldn't find anything wrong. They suggested that I talk to a mental health counselor. I resisted going until the pains started interfering with my studies. For the first time, I told someone about how much it hurt that my mother had left me and my sisters alone. How could she have loved us and done that? I also talked about my own fears about suicide, the fantasies I had about killing myself, especially now that I knew about my brother.

"I had lived in silence for so long that it defined my life. Now I understand that the feelings have to go somewhere—you can't wish them away. Sometimes the pain is so great that I can barely speak. But I know that I can't keep pretending it didn't happen, the way my father tries to do. I'm studying to be a social worker. I want to get married and have children, I want to have a normal life. The difference between my mother and me is that I will fight to be happy; I will not let myself give up."

For many survivors, healing begins when they find a comforting shoulder or a safe place to talk about their complicated and conflicting reactions to their loved one's suicide. "Everyone in my office seemed to avoid me after my wife's suicide," says Jerry, a forty-seven-year-old computer software executive from California, whose wife shot herself fifteen months ago. "People in my business are very involved in their jobs. I understand that. But when I came back to work after the funeral, no one even mentioned that my wife had died. Colleagues whom I had known for years would avert their eyes when they saw me; if we did talk, our conversation would be about the latest sales figures or basketball scores. I wanted to stand on my desk and scream: 'My wife is dead. Please, someone, acknowledge it.' I started thinking that maybe I was crazy, that I had only dreamed the suicide. It was as if the entire office was sharing a secret from which I was somehow excluded.

"One day, a salesman who was visiting from our New York office asked to speak to me. 'I heard through the grapevine that your wife recently took her life,' he said. I was floored by his honesty. 'I know what you must be going through,' he continued. 'Two years ago, my wife jumped out of our apartment window while I was shaving in the bathroom. She had suffered from depression her whole life. I never thought I would get over her suicide, but it gets easier over time. It helps to talk about it.'

"His words opened up a floodgate of tears. I started crying so hard I thought I would never be able to stop. This man, who minutes before had been a stranger, embraced me. 'Tell me about it,' he urged. The whole story about my wife's death came tumbling out of me, detail by detail. For the first time, I was even able to say the word *suicide* out loud.

"There are many suicide survivors out there—too many—and we share a special bond with each other. From the moment I realized that I was not alone, I knew I would be okay."

Like Jerry, survivors often find unexpected sources of support during the tumultuous aftermath of suicide. Yet, often we are disappointed by the absence of friends and relatives, who turn away from us as we try to cope with the disorienting repercussions of our traumatic loss.

"One of my closest friends stopped calling me after my sister's funeral," recalls Andrea, a thirty-four-year-old travel agent from Dallas. "I was in such a state of shock after Marci shot herself that my friend's disappearance seemed part of the general insanity. After several weeks, she phoned to say she was sorry but she was having a hard time accepting Marci's death. Her apology made me feel so empty. I would have really appreciated her help; instead, I assumed that she was avoiding me because she blamed me for my sister's death.

"I was amazed at who comes through for you and who doesn't. The least likely people end up offering you the greatest comfort. The day Marci killed herself, a woman from my bowling team brought over a hot casserole to my house. Even though food was the last thing on my mind, her gesture made me feel I was not alone. Afterward, she called me every day, sometimes just leaving a message on my machine if I wasn't home. She always asked how I was doing and if I needed anything. She was a very strong woman who had raised three children all by herself after her husband was killed in Vietnam. Maybe it was her own suffering that made her able to reach out to me, I don't know. Yet, I found her constant support to be very important. Her courage showed me people can go through such terrible tragedies without being destroyed.

"Marci was twenty-one when she killed herself three years ago, one week after her first wedding anniversary. She was a very private person and never talked about her feelings, not even what she thought about a movie. We came from a family where we expressed ourselves in tones and small gestures, never words. When Marci was in high school, she attempted suicide by swallowing a bottle of aspirin. She then woke up my mother, who took her to the emergency room. After the incident, Marci and my mother went to family therapy together. It was a total failure because my mother acted like a clam. She just sat there and wouldn't say a word. They eventually stopped going because Marci didn't want to go alone.

"I didn't know about Marci's overdose until she let it slip out about a year after it happened. My reaction was that her trying to kill herself made perfect sense because she was such an unhappy teenager. I never mentioned it to her again because I assumed that if she wanted to talk about it, she would bring it up herself.

"During college, Marci suffered from bouts of depression. I would call her up and she would be in bed crying. I would just let it pass, telling myself that it was not my business to intrude into her life. In her junior year, Marci dropped out of school to get married. She took a job at a medical billing company and her mood seemed more upbeat. The last conversation I had with her was about her plans for Christmas.

"On the morning Marci killed herself, she called her husband at work. She told him there was a bet going around her office about the best way to commit suicide—the best type of gun to use and the best part of your body. He answered, 'A shotgun in your mouth.' My brother-in-law is a big hunter, and Marci had a rifle he had given her for Valentine's Day. She drove home, but her husband kept all the guns in the house locked up and unloaded. My sister didn't know the combination lock for her rifle, so she used her pistol, which she kept in her own box with its own lock. The instruction book on how to load the pistol was still on the table when I went to her house that night. It is amazing to me that she had the presence of mind to follow the directions on how to put the bullets in the gun. In a way, I find some comfort in knowing that Marci had to take all these steps before she killed herself. It makes her act seem more thoughtful and less impulsive.

"Marci shot herself in what she called the 'dead animal' room of her house, a den where her husband had mounted the stuffed heads of animals he had killed. Her husband found her body when he got home from work. There was very little blood because Marci had shot herself in the mouth and there was no exit wound. She left a note for her husband that said: 'You'll be better off this way. I can't do anything right.'

"There was no autopsy because the police didn't suspect any foul play. But my mother is firmly convinced that it was murder and that a cover-up is taking place. She invents all these different scenarios—that my brother-in-law killed her, that Marci was having an affair that went wrong, that she came home unexpectedly and interrupted a robbery. Anything but the truth. I tell her that if she doesn't come to terms with the reality that my sister killed herself, she will never be able to begin mourning her. But my mother doesn't seem interested in her own life anymore. Her whole world is now consumed with finding Marci's murderer.

"After Marci's death, I couldn't sleep unless I kept the lights on. I suffered from major panic attacks, which I still have occasionally. I blamed myself for not being perceptive enough to realize that something was wrong with my sister's life. On the first anniversary of her death, I went through a period of total grief. I couldn't stop crying for weeks on end. I really missed her and craved speaking to her. I became angry at her for doing something so drastic without giving me a chance to try to help her. I still find it surprising that Marci had enough determination to kill herself but not enough to face her problems.

"My husband and I were trying to have a baby right around the time that Marci committed suicide. My first reaction was to put it off. No way did I want to bring a child into a world where such terrible things could happen. In all honesty, I was afraid that suicide might run in my family. My husband was very understanding and suggested we go to a genetic counselor at the medical center. She was absolutely wonderful, using scientific evidence to dispel my fears. I am now eight months pregnant with a baby girl. I am very hopeful for the life I plan to provide for my daughter. My sister's suicide has taught me the importance of talking about your feelings and confronting problems before they go too far. If Marci's suicide helps me to be a better mother, her death might not be as senseless as it seems."

Some survivors find great comfort in the spiritual belief that the act of suicide is a mystical occurrence that must be accepted outside conventional, preconceived concepts. "I believe that my son is not dead, that he is finally in peace somewhere else," explains Howard, a sixty-nine-year-old retired history professor from Eugene, Oregon, whose son hanged himself fifteen years ago at the age of twenty-five. "I have faith that people who commit suicide are so desperate that they don't feel emotional connections to the rest of us and must seek a place where they will belong. My son lived as full a life as possible but then came to believe he had no future. It is my hope that he has found the happiness that eluded him while he was here."

As survivors move through the healing process, one of the most difficult decisions we encounter is whether or not to reveal the true circumstances of our loved one's death. If we choose to protect our privacy by not telling the truth about the suicide, we feel guilty and ashamed; if we are honest, we run the risk of having to defend ourselves from reactions ranging from intrusive curiosity to open censure.

"My response to the question of how my husband died depends on who's asking and how I feel that day," explains Joyce, a fifty-nine-year-old mother of four who lives in an affluent suburb of New York City. "My answers include: His heart stopped. He died from depression. It's a long story. I'd rather not talk about it right now. His death was sudden. He died from unnatural causes. Then, sometimes, out of the blue, I'll find myself coming right out and saying: He committed suicide. He took his own life. He killed himself. He swallowed a bottle of Nembutal with a bottle of Absolut. He checked out.

"My husband was a prominent dentist, a perfect husband and father. We were married for almost thirty years. I had absolutely no idea that anything was wrong with him. One Friday night, five years ago, we had tickets for the theater. I had spent the day shopping in the city, and we had planned to meet at our favorite French restaurant before the show. He wasn't there when I arrived so I figured that he had been delayed in traffic. After about an hour, I called our home and his office but only got both machines. I then paged him on his beeper. There was still no response—this was totally out of character for him.

"The train ride home seemed to take forever. I called my husband again from the station; still no one answered. When I arrived home, there were two police cars parked in front of my house. I knew he was dead. The police told me that the cleaning lady at his office had found my husband's body. I automatically assumed that he'd had a heart attack because he suffered from high blood pressure. Then, the police told me they had found a handwritten note and bottles of pills and vodka on his desk. When they said the preliminary cause of death was suicide, I heard these howls starting to come out of me. I felt like the person in the Munch painting 'The Scream.' The police must have called my son, who lived nearby. He's a doctor, so he was able to give me a shot to calm me down. It knocked me out for several hours.

"The next day I called the police to get the keys to my husband's office. At first they wouldn't release them, but I had my lawyer call and they relented. My husband's favorite blue sports jacket was draped on the back of his desk chair. There was an ashtray filled with cigarette butts, even though he had stopped smoking fifteen years ago. I also had my lawyer get a copy of the suicide note from the police. It said he loved me, that my love had kept him going, but he didn't know what else to do.

"For months on end, I would retrace the events of those days. I would go over every detail of every minute, searching for a clue I might have missed. Now, after all these years, my recollections are starting to become fuzzy. I know it's a natural process but it makes me feel sad, as if I'm starting to forget him.

"Everyone tells you not to make any decisions during the first year. It is very wise advice. I was so numb and confused. I wanted to sell my house, move to California, give away the artwork my husband and I had carefully collected throughout our marriage. Basically, I just wanted to run away. Instead, I started going to intensive therapy and joined a widow's support group. I was the only member whose husband had committed suicide. I was surprised to discover that the other women, all of whom had lost their husbands to natural causes, were also angry at having been left. My anger was the greatest, however, because my husband had died knowingly and willingly.

"After my husband's death, I felt that I was the focus of gossip. I sensed that there was this question about my integrity as a wife. I felt very pointed-out, judged, and objectified. My friends gradually stopped including me in their plans. I don't know if they dropped me because I was a single woman or because of my husband's suicide or both. All I know is that when I was invited to two weddings of the children of people who had been my closest friends, once I was seated with three elderly widows and the other time I was put at the children's table. My circle of friends—the couples—were sitting together.

"Two years after my husband killed himself, I decided to find a job. I was always a wife and mother who was fairly well off financially so I had never worked in my life. But I knew I had to do something for myself. I went to temp agencies, but I was so nervous I couldn't even read the instructions for the spelling test. Then I did something I consider very courageous. I enrolled in a reentry program for displaced homemakers at the local YMCA. There were all types of women there—from different racial, ethnic, and economic backgrounds. Yet, we all bonded and helped each other. At the end of the program, I was chosen by the other women to give the graduation speech. I had never done any public speaking, although I had helped my husband with his presentations at professional conferences. I was terrified, but I had the audience laughing and crying. It made me feel so good about myself.

"I now work at an entry-level job at an insurance company. I sold my house and moved to a condominium apartment in another town. All my friends are new. I find it difficult to go out with men, however, because I still feel defensive about my husband's death. Recently, I dated a man whom I found very attractive. When I finally told him the truth about the suicide, he became very uncomfortable. He kept on trying to find out what was *really* wrong with my marriage, why my husband *really* killed himself.

"I truly wanted to grow old with my husband. I have these fantasies of our holding hands and being together. I would have done anything to save him if I'd known he was depressed. Since his death, I have had to learn what my own capabilities are. Even if I do marry again, I will never give up knowing how strong I am. Although part of me died with my husband, I have faith that I will be able to love again."

As we begin to put our lives together, survivors gradually find that the acute rawness of our pain is replaced by a dull ache of regret for the uncompleted lives of the people we have lost. In our moving on, we discover that we still have the capacity to laugh and love, even to be concerned about the ordinary worries of the everyday world.

Kelly, the young social worker from Houston whose twin brother shot himself almost one year ago, told me she was engaged to be married when her brother committed suicide. A large wedding had been planned for several weeks after her brother's funeral, and she did not know if she should cancel the arrangements.

"I went to the rabbi for advice," she said. "He told me that when two processions meet, the funeral procession waits for the wedding procession. So I went ahead with our big wedding. Although I was mourning my brother, I celebrated my marriage and love for my husband with all the joy it deserved."

Like Kelly, I, too, was confused by achieving the delicate balance between going forward and not forgetting. In the process of resuming my life and forging a new one, I came to understand that life does come before death, as a wedding must move ahead of a funeral. Over time, the rich memories of the many years I spent with Harry started to reemerge, as in a faded photograph that suddenly regains the sharpness of its lost images. As the clarity returned, the chaos receded: My healing had begun.

Effect on
Families

> *"We believe that suicide occurs in all types of families:*
> *the functional and the dysfunctional; the very good,*
> *the not so good, and the just good enough."*

—Edward Dunne and Karen Dunne-Maxim,
Suicide and Its Aftermath: Understanding and Counseling the Survivors

efore Harry died, I was aware of suicide from a comfortable distance. I would read stories about rock stars overdosing or politicians shooting themselves or children of celebrities jumping out windows. I would hear news of high school classmates or casual acquaintances unexpectedly taking their lives. I would see thoughtful essays exploring the suicides of prominent writers and artists. These startling accounts of interrupted lives and early deaths seemed to have a faraway, almost unreal quality. I could not imagine a desperation so unyielding that ending your life became the only possible refuge.

Although suicide is almost universally condemned, it is also admired for its boldness and audacity. Killing yourself is considered dramatic; there is a certain cachet to knocking on death's door instead of waiting for it to sneak up on you when you are not looking. Yet, suicide is not a self-contained act: For those of us who are left behind, the violent disruption of life's natural order throws us off balance, leaving us shaken and confused.

We are also afraid. We are told about a possible "suicide gene" that can be passed down from generation to generation. We are informed that after our exposure to a loved one's suicide, we are more psychologically receptive to consider it as a viable option for ourselves. Survivors learn that our chances of killing ourselves are now significantly greater, with rates estimated at up to 400 percent higher than those of the general public.

"The idea of suicide as a solution to a problem often becomes implanted in the mind of the survivor," states Dr. Edward Dunne in *Suicide and Its Aftermath: Understanding and Counseling the Survivors*. "Survivors have had the 'veil' of death lifted and are forced to confront existential reality. . . . They view the suicide as a way to handle a difficult interpersonal, financial, or legal problem or situation. What's more, the closeness of the survivor's relationship to the deceased promotes an openness to options suggested by the deceased."

According to the National Institute of Mental Health, one out of four people who attempt suicide has a family member who also tried to commit suicide. Current research suggests that suicide tends to run in families, possibly as a result of such genetic factors as depression, or because the family member serves as a role model.

After Harry's death, I was terrified of the suicidal images that suddenly crowded my thoughts. Killing myself had now joined the list of answers to the multiple choice question of what to do if life became too frightening or overwhelming. My husband's experience confirmed how easy it could be: If you want to leave, nothing can stop you.

"Suicide is part of my family legacy," says Lisa, a forty-one-year-old director of a homeless shelter in Cleveland, Ohio. "Twenty years ago, my brother hung himself in the backyard of the house where we grew up. He was in his junior year of high school and had just been elected president of his class. I was away at college and my older sister found him. Eight years later, my father killed himself with carbon monoxide from his car. He left a note for his remaining six children saying that he blamed himself for my brother's suicide and he hoped his death would break the cycle of self-destruction that had already appeared in our family. Even after many years of therapy, there is a part of me that still believes my family must be cursed.

"We came from a nice suburban household outside of Cleveland. After my brother's suicide, my parents got divorced. I went to a counselor at my college, who told me I should forget about my family and live my own life. I just felt numb at his response. There was no place to go for help.

"My reaction was to throw myself into my work. I was on the dean's list for the next four semesters and graduated with honors. Even though I was successful, I started on a course of progressive and intermittent drug and alcohol use. On the day my father killed himself, I stopped all drinking and drugs.

"I knew my brother had been depressed. He would call me

up to ask me to take a drive with him to the lake, then he wouldn't say a word the whole time. He started to get worse and worse. Finally, my father took him to a psychiatrist, who gave him pills. He killed himself the day he was supposed to start his medication.

"Both my father and brother drank. I understand that alcoholism is a terminal disease where you end up dead. But my father stopped drinking six months before he killed himself, using his anger to complete the act. My mother is a very religious Roman Catholic and has found great comfort in her faith. Both my father and brother had formal church funeral services and burials. But I'm bothered by that. I was taught that suicide is a mortal sin. Yet, if you kill yourself, all seems to be forgiven.

"I'm furious at my father. His selfish act has only continued the self-destruction in our family, not stopped it. On the way to my father's funeral, my sister, the one who found my brother, had a nervous breakdown. She began screaming, threatening to kill herself. We had to commit her to the hospital that night, and she's been in and out of mental institutions ever since. My youngest brother is the only one of us who has a normal life. He explains his escape from the dysfunction of our family by saying that he was watching from the balcony while the rest of us were sitting in the front row.

"I once heard a psychiatrist say that suicide is the only way that someone dies by choice. I disagree with him. Suicide is a perception of choice. Since my father's death, I constantly have to fight against my own suicidal feelings. I'm in therapy and attend many different support groups. I have told my best friend to admit me to a hospital immediately if I start talking about killing myself. I am doing everything possible to keep myself alive."

As we struggle to put our lives back together, survivors must deal not only with the chaos that suicide leaves behind but also with the uncertainty of its future effects. Even as we begin to understand that our loved ones killed themselves in a desperate attempt to end their pain, we often feel that their anguish has not been extinguished but simply passed on to us.

"I'm terrified at the idea that one day I will kill myself like my sister and father before me," says Caitlan, a thirty-seven-year-old fashion designer from New York City. "Ten years ago, my sister took an overdose of painkillers after her husband left her for another woman. My mother never recovered from the suicide. She became more and more isolated, holding herself back from my father and me. Four years after my sister's death, my mother was diagnosed with lymphoma; she died three years later.

"My father, whom I always thought of as being the strong one in the family, started talking about killing himself after my mother died. He began calling me all the time, saying that life wasn't worth it anymore. I found myself putting a distance between us. I was the only family member left and I was afraid that he was becoming too dependent on me. He would tell me that he was lonely and ask me to come visit him. But I didn't reach out to him, just the opposite. The more insistent he became, the more I made up excuses not to see him.

"Ten months after my mother died, my father shot himself in the bedroom of his house. I feel so guilty—I'm the only member in my family who has survived, yet I couldn't save my sister, mother, or father. I've just begun therapy but I'm totally overwhelmed. Is my family damned? Will I also want to kill myself one day? Is suicide genetic? I wrestle with all these questions day and night. I feel crazy because I can't get these obsessive thoughts out of my head."

Like Caitlan, many survivors are threatened by the possibility of an increased risk of suicide once a family member takes his or her life. "My only wish is that I die a normal death," says Mike, a graduate student at the University of Pennsylvania. "My grandfather died by accidentally shooting himself while cleaning his gun. I was very young but I remember how my parents talked about his death, as if they were hiding something. Then, two years ago, my father was killed when his car hit a telephone pole. He was always such a careful driver, and I was bothered about his accident. I guess I'll never know if my father and my grandfather killed themselves. If it's true, then I feel there's really no hope for me. I want my death to be clear-cut—I just want to get sick and die. I would not want any child of mine to be burdened with the same kind of doubts that I am living with."

Some survivors, however, view the suicide of a family member as a courageous response to an intolerable situation. "Both my dad and his brother were brilliant men who worried about their lack of success," says Lukas, a thirty-two-year-old musician from Los Angeles. "My uncle killed himself before I was born. My dad, who died last year from stomach cancer, suffered from deep depression his whole life. He was either on medication or in hospitals throughout most of my childhood. I believe that the only reason he didn't kill himself was because he was too depressed. To me, suicide is an incredibly brave act. People who are able to end their lives are action-oriented—they are able to cut to the chase.

"My dad talked to me a lot about his brother's suicide. He traced his clinical depression from the rejection and trauma he felt after his brother died. When I was in high school, my dad was so bad that he couldn't even get up in the morning. He was hospitalized for electroshock therapy but nothing seemed to work. He talked about suicide not as a threat, only as a way of stopping how he was feeling. When I would see the way he was suffering, I began to think that death would be welcome.

"I don't know if my dad made any suicide attempts during this period. I think what might have held him back was that he didn't want me to be as affected by his suicide as he was by his brother's. He began living through me and became totally involved with helping me to achieve success with my music. I have never felt so emotionally together in my life as I did at that time. I saw how much my dad needed me and how strong I had to be in order to help keep him going. I also came to believe that if my father killed himself, it would be bolder and more courageous than how he was living. Now, I still agree with that, although the feelings aren't so pure and unshaded.

"My dad died at a point in his life when he was mentally at peace. When he developed stomach cancer, he was in a lot of pain. He talked about his fear of dying but said he now realized how precious life was. But he also insisted on putting himself on a morphine drip and teaching me how to administer it in case the doctors or nurses wouldn't do it. I had no problem with that. It was done and it was a courageous act. My father was incredibly brave as he faced the enormity of death.

"Suicide is not an option for me because my mother is around and I would be afraid of what my death would do to her. Yet, sometimes I think I would be dead by now if I had access to a gun, even in spite of my mother. I'm aware that depression associated with suicide could be genetic. I will just have to face it if it happens."

Although Lukas was at peace with his decision to assist his father in ending his life, other survivors experience enormous conflict about their role in helping a loved one commit suicide. Because it seems almost impossible to distinguish the symptoms of depression from the symptoms of an incurable or painful disease, many survivors describe persistent feelings of doubt and guilt after participating in the suicide of a family member.

"I'll never know if my brother really wanted to die or if he felt that he was being a burden to the family," says Angela, a twenty-seven-year-old flight attendant from Miami. "Kenny had AIDS and had been hospitalized five times in the last two years. He told us that he planned to kill himself when his weight dropped below eighty pounds. Six months ago, it did. Over the years, he had amassed a whole array of sleeping pills and painkillers. Kenny wanted us all around him when he died—my mother, brother, and his best friend. I was always uncomfortable with the way he planned his suicide. Why was he really ending his life? He knew that his illness had been a tremendous financial, physical, and emotional responsibility for my family. Was he leaving for his sake or for ours? Was Kenny's suicide 'rational'? My mother says that we made the right decision because we helped Kenny end his suffering. I've been thinking about it all the time but I still don't feel comfortable about what happened."

Every family member reacts to the suicide of a loved one in his or her own individual manner: from anger to admiration, from identification to denial. Dr. Edward Dunne likens the suicide of his brother, Tim, to a meteorite that crashed into his family, sending each member into different and separate orbits of mourning. "Suicide destroys the original fabric of the family, forcing a reintegration of the survivors," he says. "The pace at which individual family members are ready and able to do this will vary, necessitating individual interventions."

Donald is a fifty-eight-year-old salesman from Kansas City whose wife killed herself one year ago with a combination of alcohol and tranquilizers. "My family was ripped apart by her death," he explains. "My daughter, who found her, blames her suicide on my constantly being away from home. When I tell her that her mother had a drinking problem, she says I'm just trying to make excuses for my behavior. It's really a myth that people pull together in a crisis. My wife's suicide exposed all the problems that already existed between me and my children. Whatever fault lines were there just became deeper and more entrenched."

With any suicide, there is often a need to blame someone other than the person who has taken his or her life. In teenage suicides, the finger is most often pointed at the youngster's parents for their apparent failure to keep their child alive. Ann Landers, in her nationally syndicated column, offered an extremely compassionate reply to a mother who had written about how devastated she felt when people asked her why she had done nothing to prevent her young daughter from killing herself.

"You do not owe an explanation to anyone who is so insensitive (or mean-spirited) that he or she would ask a mother of a suicide why someone didn't reach out to her child before it was too late," Ms. Landers advised. "There are times when the best response is a spell of cold, stinging silence, followed by, 'Why would anyone ask a mother such a question?' "

Youth suicide is a growing social problem in the United States, with the number of young people killing themselves increasing every year. According to the National Institute of Mental Health, suicide is the third major cause of death among all adolescents and the second major cause of death among college students. Males are six times more likely to kill themselves than females, although females have a higher rate of suicide attempts.

As part of an alarming national trend, recent statistics from the Centers for Disease Control and Prevention reveal a 120 percent increase in the suicide rate among children ages ten to fourteen. From 1980 to 1992, the rate among white boys in this age group went up 86 percent, while the rate for black boys increased by 300 percent. There was a 233 percent rise in suicide rates for white girls and a 100 percent increase for black girls. The use of guns figured prominently in these numbers: In 1992, firearm-related deaths accounted for 65 percent of all suicides among people under twenty-five. For young people between the ages of fifteen and nineteen, firearm-related suicides were responsible for 81 percent of the increase in the overall rates between 1980 and 1992.

Research describes how adolescents become curious and even excited when suicide is talked about in heroic ways as opposed to being characterized as a result of mental illness. This romanticizing of death often accounts for copycat suicides among young people and outbreaks of cluster suicides in schools and communities.

"The suicide of a student touches everyone—students, teachers, administrators, and support staff—stirring up the same kind of emotions and conflicts that affect all survivors of suicide," write Frederick Lamb and Karen Dunne-Maxim in *Suicide and Its Aftermath: Understanding and Counseling the Survivors.* "In a very real sense the school community is itself a survivor, requiring the same sensitive support and help that individuals do after such a tragedy." The authors stress that following the suicide of a young person, the focus of attention must be on the needs of the living, the survivors. They recommend that nothing be done to glamorize or dramatize a suicide, but doing nothing can be as dangerous as doing too much. They also emphasize that students in a school cannot be helped until the faculty is also counseled.

The suicide of a child can tear apart the foundation of trust and mutual responsibility that is necessary for a marriage to survive. The Samaritans of New York, a suicide prevention group in New York City, report that 70 percent of the parents of teenage suicides eventually divorce.

"My wife and I separated several months after our sixteen-year-old daughter jumped in front of a train together with her best friend," says Vic, a fifty-four-year-old pharmacist from a small town in Wyoming. "I really regret that we couldn't work things out. We virtually stopped talking to each other after the suicide. We were like zombies. I don't think I have spoken to my wife in the past four years, although I know she must be in agony. It seems funny that she would understand how I feel more than anyone in the world, yet we can't share any of our feelings about our daughter's death."

For many parents, guilt over their children's suicide is compounded by the real or perceived prejudgment that they are responsible for the actions of their children. "I just accepted it when people blamed me for Billy's death because I believed it to be true," recalls Emmy, a forty-one-year-old physician's assistant from Santa Fe whose fourteen-year-old son shot himself five years ago. "After Billy killed himself, I had the strong sensation that I had also died. I was convinced that I had been in a car accident and was lingering between two worlds. My identity was so caught up with my son that after his death I had only a slim connection to life. Eventually, the numbness started wearing off and I realized I wasn't dead after all. But then a wave of terror came over me. I was alive and the pain would never end; the nightmare was here. How was I going to get through the rest of my life?

"It took several weeks for my sensations to start to become distinct. The state of shock protects you from taking in the full extent of devastation, so you don't totally lose your mind. You know something disastrous has happened but not the full impact.

"When I went back to work, I felt so disassociated. I didn't belong there. Everyone knew I wasn't myself and it seemed as if people were patronizing me. There was this normal world going on around me but I couldn't assimilate it. It only highlighted my disorientation. A couple of months before Billy killed himself, one of the nurses in my office died a very painful death from lung cancer. When I visited her in the hospital, she told me she had very seriously considered ending her life but then thought, What's the point of doing the inevitable? It's going to happen anyway. But what does a young boy like Billy know about that?

"A couple of months after Billy died, I went out for the first time with my husband and sister. We went to the movies, then to dinner. I had an overwhelming feeling of horror the entire evening. I was trying to engage in conversation and enjoy the food but the horror inside my mind was so startling. I could hear myself talking but it was from a distance. Everything was so meaningless: I was like the walking dead, the emotionally dead.

"After Billy's suicide, I became estranged from my husband. Our son's death was not a shared loss, it was an individual loss. He was my son yet he was my husband's son also. We talked about it all the time but it divided us as a couple. I thought about suicide a lot. I wanted to get in my car and slam it into a wall. I would ask my husband if he wanted to have a suicide pact with me so we could die together. He would get very angry when I talked like that. Then I would imagine killing myself alone—after all, it was between me and my son.

"Billy shot himself in the basement of our home. My husband found him when he came home from work. When he called me at the office with the news, I drove directly to my sister's house, which was nearby. I never set foot in my house again. We stayed with my sister for a month before renting another house in the neighborhood. I didn't care about my surroundings. This wasn't my home, just a place to stay. Both my husband and I started neglecting our responsibilities to our marriage. We stopped cleaning the house, buying food, toilet paper, soap. We would bathe with shampoo, that's how dysfunctional we were.

"Gradually, I started wondering if the loss of our son was greater than our love for each other. I started to fight to reestablish our life together. I knew that if our marriage was going to survive, we would have to make room for each other. I had two battles: I had to survive Billy's suicide and also prevent the complete destruction of our marriage. We were each carrying around our own blame about our son's death—two people, both of whom were one hundred percent guilty.

"Six months after Billy's suicide, a coworker told me about a suicide support group. I was completely hostile about sharing my tragedy with total strangers. I didn't care about their losses and I was ashamed of mine. I was resistant, but my husband really wanted to go. After the meetings, he would be relieved, while I would be angry. Yet, I continued attending, for his sake, as I told myself.

"There was a couple at one of the meetings who had lost a daughter five years earlier. I was totally disgusted—I thought, Five years down the road and they're still going to meetings. Obviously, this doesn't work. But then I started listening to people who were just beginning to go to meetings after many years of suffering in silence. It was even more terrifying to think you could live a 'normal' life and then be hit with all these feelings you had been repressing for so long. The fear it could happen to me made me stick it out.

"At first, I didn't relate to the other stories. Eventually, though, I started listening to the other people and caring for them. I saw their horror in all kinds of manifestations, with a common link running through the different variations. I began noting patterns in the process of survival: the numbness, the horrendous guilt, the fear of becoming suicidal and insane. This was a prevalent fear among the group members, that the act of suicide was a contagious disease and we would contract it from our loved ones. The similarities between us were so strong. I have to admit I was unprepared for the realization that I could have such a powerful connection to people I didn't know.

"In the groups, you can achieve some degree of objectivity concerning others. I forgave everyone and wanted them to forgive themselves. But I couldn't find the same compassion for myself, because I knew that I had committed the worst crime by allowing my child to die. Yet, the people in the groups were describing the same emotions I was experiencing. I began to see how suicide affected other people and this gave me the distance to understand my own feelings. Before, it had been a nightmare where I couldn't wake up. Slowly, I realized that I would not feel this way forever.

"The support groups were essential to me on a personal level. They did not work, however, for my husband and me as a couple. We were helped with our individual losses as a mother and father, but not as a husband and wife. We decided to go to marriage counseling for awhile, but that didn't seem to help very much either.

"My husband wanted to have another child right away. He wanted to be a parent again. But I felt very alienated by that. It seemed to have nothing to do with our marriage, just my husband's desire to be a father. I was not ready for a child because I felt we were living in chaos. I was also deeply hurt that my husband's need to be a parent appeared more important than his being a husband to me.

"What really seemed to be a turning point is that we got a

dog two years after Billy's suicide. The dog helped us redis-
cover all the roles and responsibilities of nurturing that we had
lost. Basically, we had stopped caring for ourselves and each
other after Billy died. The primary function of being a parent
is to nurture; we both still had the feelings but nowhere to put
them. The dog was sickly and we shared in the responsibility
of bringing him back to health. This was an important first
step, because my husband and I started being concerned about
the same thing. We also began to show feelings again to each
other, emotions that we thought had been obliterated. The
dog put us back in the role of caretakers.

"We are now trying to have a child. Both of us want this
very much. I know that my husband will be a responsible and
caring father, like he was with Billy. I also believe I will be a
good mother even though there are times when I'm afraid
something will go wrong again. Both my husband and I have
worked hard against very strong odds to put our marriage
back together. I am thankful that we really didn't die with
Billy but allowed ourselves to have this second chance."

Like Emmy, survivors must constantly fight to put the
pieces of our lives back together and reestablish our own iden-
tities. Often, it seems an impossible task. Several years ago,
when the sale of Harry's medical office fell through once again
and my financial situation was on the verge of crashing, my
resolve to keep myself above water in spite of my husband's
suicide began to desert me. I was convinced that my life would
never get better. It seemed as if I were on an inevitable spiral
downward, that hope was an illusion and faith an empty
dream.

This is how Harry felt, I told myself. I found myself reso-
nating with his despair. My escalating depression connected
me closer and closer to my husband. I confided my fantasies of

self-destruction to my therapist; I began retreating from my friends. What's the use? I would ask myself over and over. Life did not seem worth the effort anymore.

As my mood went from gray to black, I came home one day to a message on my answering machine. An important project of mine had just been sold. Jubilation swept over me. Not only would my work be published, I now had an extra cushion of money to keep me going until I could try once again to sell the office. Within seconds, my despair evaporated. I was filled with plans for the future.

Weeks later, I was having dinner with a friend who has battled depression her entire life. I told her the story of what I had recently experienced, how I could now understand what she must go through when she is racked with feelings of hopelessness and despair.

"No, Carla," she corrected me. "When you are truly depressed, even the best news in the world cannot make you feel better."

"How is that possible?" I asked incredulously. It seemed inconceivable that desperation could be so fixed that the inevitable changes and movement in our lives would not shake it loose.

And then I realized the difference. Although suicidal fantasies might help us make it through the bad nights—there is always a way out if things become too intolerable—most people do not want to die. Survivors have walked through the fire without being engulfed, propelled forward by our courage and will. For those of us who have been left behind, the legacy of suicide lies not in reconciling ourselves to inevitable defeat but in recognizing that our spirit of survival remains both resilient and intact.

Getting Help

*"The death of a significant other by suicide is a stressor
of unparalleled magnitude in most people's lives, and
even the most psychologically mature individual may
encounter difficulty in responding to it."*

—Edward Dunne,
Suicide and Its Aftermath: Understanding and Counseling the Survivors

We start out as perfect strangers in a group. Eighteen people go around the room telling their stories and we are linked. We have been there. We all deal differently with suicide—some have rage, some have sorrow, some have utter forgiveness and understanding. We all have loss.

It is seven months since my husband killed himself; I have been coming to these support meetings for six months, half of one year. I have also been going to individual therapy twice a week. I am reading every book possible on why people kill themselves. I continue to search through the literature—both popular and professional—for publications directed to those of us who have lost a loved one to suicide. Although our needs have been described as the "greatest among all groups affected by suicidal behavior" (John McIntosh, *Suicide and Its Aftermath: Understanding and Counseling the Survivors*), the material available to us offering support and assistance is remarkably meager.

I am also surprised that in New York City, with a population of eight million people, there are so few support groups for suicide survivors. I attend the meetings held by Samaritans, an organization primarily concerned with suicide prevention. Led by volunteers, these groups are offered free of charge two evenings each month. At some meetings, the room is crowded with almost twenty people; other times, fewer than ten of us show up. Where is everyone else, I wonder.

Ever since Harry died, I have found great comfort in these groups. Although I am fortunate to have a therapist who can discuss suicide without getting tangled up in rigid orthodoxy or frightened by the relentless talk of death, the meetings satisfy my intense desire to connect with others who are going through the same experience I am. My therapist is enthusiastic about the groups; she is not threatened by the "self-help" nature of their structure but views them as an essential ingredient in my healing process.

Getting help is imperative for all survivors of suicide—whether we find it through support groups, individual therapy, family counseling, or spiritual comfort. Unfortunately, the interest of the mental health profession centers on the people who commit suicide, not on those of us who are left behind to deal with its consequences.

"Little has been done by the current mental health system

in terms of developing treatment models for working with survivors either individually or as family systems," writes Dr. McIntosh. "In fact, survivors themselves have brought the issue to the fore and have pointed out the inadequacies of the mental health system in dealing with this issue."

Not every person who suffers the loss of a loved one to suicide needs a powerful intervention to deal with their problems, according to Dr. Edward Dunne. "There are plenty of people who do fine without therapy," he explains. "If they're wounded, they heal. Yet, others need a great deal of help." Dr. Dunne also points out that some people who have experienced the suicide of someone close to them often do not seek help from the mental health profession because they are angry at the profession for having been unable to save the life of the deceased, or they fear that they will be stigmatized as a mentally ill person if they seek professional counseling.

"I tried going to a psychiatrist right after my sister died, but it was a terrible experience," explains Lois, a forty-year-old investment banker from Boston. "The doctor was highly regarded for his work in the field of suicide, but he seemed more interested in the circumstances surrounding my sister's suicide than in how I was feeling. It rapidly became apparent to me that he considered my sister to be his patient, not me. Every time I talked about my guilt or the nightmares that were keeping me awake, he would bring the topic back to her. It was all about my sister's pain, not mine.

"I was in a state of shock when I went to see this doctor, so it was impossible for me to determine if the problem was with me or with him. I felt incapable of making an objective assessment of him. During my third session, I told him I felt like killing myself. His immediate response was that if this were true, he would have to institutionalize me. Instead of helping me with my suicidal feelings and severe panic attacks, he was punishing me by threatening to commit me to a mental hospital.

"This psychiatrist did not tell me that my reaction was typical among survivors. There was no reassurance. I knew I could never mention again that I felt like killing myself—the reason I was going to him in the first place. Ironically, suicide had become a taboo subject.

"Instead of talking to me, the doctor put me on Prozac. But I had a bad reaction—the medication filled me with a constant feeling of foreboding. Then he told me the pills weren't working because I wasn't 'depressed' enough. This after he threatened to put me in an institution! I constantly felt as if he were blaming me for not getting better. Finally, after three months, he told me there was no purpose in my continuing treatment. He didn't even recommend another therapist. I was very angry and I wouldn't pay the bill for my last session.

"At that point, I decided to go to my general practitioner, a doctor whom I trusted very much. He told me I was depressed and had every right to be. He put me on Tofranil, an older, well-known antidepressant. He also recommended that I join a support group.

"I could not have survived without the groups. The people there were the only ones who could understand the pain, guilt, horror, and fear I was experiencing. We all had self-destructive thoughts after the suicide—I wasn't crazy after all. I also felt compassion for everyone at the meetings. I cried for them and cried for myself. Once I realized there was still a part of me that could care for others, I knew I would be okay."

The intense interaction among participants is what distinguishes suicide support groups from twelve-step programs, according to Rick, a volunteer who has facilitated survivors groups in San Francisco for the past five years. "The format I use in the meetings has evolved through trial and error," he explains. "We sit in a circle, with each person giving a brief introduction: first name, who was lost, when it was, and how it happened. I then ask the people who are attending for the first time to begin, because they usually have an urgent need to talk. The rest of the group reaches out to them by describing their own experiences and how they are feeling. The new people realize they are not alone with their nightmare. By comparing their situations with others', they also begin to understand that they don't have a monopoly on pain.

"In all my years of conducting these groups, I must say that I have never heard any participant express judgment against another person. The members of the groups are always very forgiving—of everyone else but themselves. Eventually, when they realize that they do not blame the others, they stop blaming themselves.

"Comparison is the best medicine. There is such an air of mystery surrounding suicide. People are looking for closure and answers, wanting to know what has *really* happened. This is especially difficult with suicide because we can't ask the people who killed themselves why they did it. The one common denominator among the people who come to the meetings is pain. With some, recovery is slower and the bitterness deeper; others are able to compartmentalize their feelings.

"The groups never become depressing to me, just the opposite. When I was younger, my life was troubled. Along the way, I was helped by different people who literally redirected my course. It is very important for someone to be there to listen. I believe that life is a journey and there should be sentinels along the way to hold out their hands to you. You, in turn, should then hold out your hand to others. There is enough real suffering. If someone has been there, he or she can help alleviate another person's pain. I will do that for the rest of my life."

Some survivors are uneasy about seeking out support groups because of the personal and public stigma surrounding suicide. "I thought everyone there would look like crazed maniacs," relates Marie, the wife of the California politician who shot himself six years ago. "It took me one and a half years to go to my first meeting. I felt like damaged goods and didn't want to be associated with other people in my situation. No way did I want to join a circle of losers. To my surprise, the people in the group were normal human beings who were dazed and hurt, not freaky. Within a short time, I grew to respect and care for them.

"My first meeting really blew me away. People were throwing around the S word so casually—*suicide* this and *suicide* that. To me, *suicide* was like a curse word; I would only say my husband killed himself, never that he committed suicide. I had felt so isolated but, all of a sudden, I saw that there were other people who knew exactly what I was going through.

"I attended the meetings for more than a year. Now I go occasionally—on the anniversary of my husband's death, during the Christmas holidays, on my wedding anniversary. I think the people who go to these groups have a lot of courage. When someone says to me that my husband must have been very brave to take his own life, I get furious. The real heroes of this drama are those of us who are trying to put our lives back together, piece by piece. We are the ones who have to face straightening up the mess and making sense of the insanity. We cry, we laugh, we hang on to each other for dear life, but we do survive, thank God."

There are many excellent suicide support groups throughout the United States and Canada (see listings, Chapter 18), and their numbers are growing. These peer support groups are offered free of charge and are organized on a community, grassroots level. Survivors should be wary, however, of any group that is conducted by someone with no personal connection to suicide or with no ties to other local groups concerned with providing support services for people who have lost a loved one to suicide.

"The process of recovery, or learning to trust again, is hard enough without being exploited and betrayed by someone who passes himself off as wanting to help," says Maureen, a fifty-one-year-old corporate lawyer from Washington, DC. "When my father died two years ago, I was completely devastated. He was a well-known journalist who shot himself because he feared that he was developing the first signs of Alzheimer's disease. When a friend of mine told me about a support group run by a psychologist, I jumped at the chance to be able to talk to other people who were in my same situation.

"When I called the doctor to find out details about where the meetings were held, he told me he would first have to interview me in his private office. Even though I was still numb—my father had killed himself only five weeks before—it struck me as unusual that I had to be 'accepted' into the group. When I went for my appointment with him, he began asking extremely specific and personal questions about the exact circumstances surrounding my father's suicide. During the interview, which lasted almost two hours, he took copious notes. He prefaced our talk by stating that everything I was telling him was strictly confidential.

"The doctor had been conducting his support group for more than a year. The meetings were held in the classroom of a local high school; even so, he asked for a ten dollar 'donation' from each participant to cover his expenses. Many times, people in the group would ask him why he was taking time out from his practice to do this, and he would always answer that he felt a lot of empathy and concern for us, that he truly wanted to 'help' us.

"One day, around six months after I started going to his group, I was reading an article in one of those throwaway newspapers about how some Gulf War veterans are suffering from post-traumatic stress disorder. The reporter included a quote from the doctor, citing him as an expert, based on a book he was writing about suicide survivors. I literally began shaking. This man had not only lied to us about his reasons for holding the meetings but also was betraying our confidence to make a quick buck for himself.

"I immediately phoned the doctor, who confirmed that, yes, he was hoping to publish a book about the experiences of the group members. When I asked him why he had not informed us about his plans beforehand, he answered that he did not want us to become 'self-conscious' during the meetings. He added that no one would be recognizable since he was writing a fictionalized account from a suicide survivor's point of view. Remember, this man is not a suicide survivor himself, so all his research was gathered from group members who, in addition to being ripped off financially, were also being exploited emotionally.

"During our phone call, his attitude was both cavalier and arrogant. I guess he thought because there is such a silence surrounding suicide, the members of the group would just swallow his betrayal and shut up. But we didn't. We lodged complaints against him with governmental agencies and professional societies. We also made sure that his use of our pain and anguish for his own monetary gain was communicated to other survivor groups in the area.

"The effect on me personally was extremely destructive. I

am in private therapy and, as my psychiatrist put it, this experience substantially undermined my healing process. It was even more painful for me to witness the reactions of the other group members to this man's breach of faith. People I had come to know and care for were crushed by his behavior. One had to return to a therapist's care after months of relative peace; another began to suffer panic attacks on a regular basis.

"This doctor's actions clearly violated the ethical considerations of a psychologist's relationship with his clients. He abused the trust of those of us who thought he was offering a safe place for sharing the pain we were hiding from the rest of the world. I truly believe that he was counting on the very shame that suicide survivors suffer to ensure that his actions would not be made public. Yet, even though I fought back, the whole episode affected me greatly. Eventually, I joined another support group but I still feel slightly wary. I hope that our experience is an isolated one. Suicide survivors have been to hell and back—we should not be made to feel even more vulnerable than we are."

Dr. Dunne believes that the challenge to the therapist treating a person who has lost a loved one to suicide is two-fold: (1) to examine his or her own attitudes about suicide and survivors as a means of eliminating any vestiges of archaic attitudes and beliefs, which can seriously undermine the therapeutic work, and (2) to become aware of the need survivors have for competent yet compassionate handling by mental health professionals.

Yet, even with such enlightened experts as Dr. Dunne beginning to reshape the present attitude toward mourning a death by suicide, there still exists a widespread resentment among many survivors against the mental health profession for its perceived insensitivity or even ignorance in offering appropriate support. In addition, survivors often feel their needs are overlooked because the emphasis on suicide research and prevention within the medical community overshadows their concerns.

"I recently went to a conference for suicide survivors sponsored by a national health care organization," describes Seth, a thirty-seven-year-old basketball coach from New Haven whose older brother shot himself last year. "All these so-called experts were on stage talking about *their* research, *their* insights, *their* experiences. The survivors were sitting in the audience, most of us still raw with our live-wire emotions, listening to speaker after speaker drone on about scientific studies, statistics, and psychological observations about why people kill themselves. One doctor even asked us—her captive audience—for contributions to help her continue with her research. We each sat there, lost in our separateness, asking ourselves what the hell these people were talking about. Finally, the only survivor on the program gave her presentation. As she related her compelling and moving story about losing her son, I began to cry. At last someone was talking about what I was feeling, not what my brother might have been feeling.

"Later, we broke up into support groups according to our relationship to the person we had lost. Around fifteen people showed up for the sibling meeting. We began by going around the circle, introducing ourselves and giving a short synopsis of what had happened. One of the people in the circle introduced himself as a psychologist specializing in depression. He said that he was there as an observer because he wanted to gain insights from our experiences so he could better understand his suicidal patients. I was incensed and insulted. Once again, the focus was shifting away from us. I spoke up, saying that I didn't pay sixty dollars to come to this conference so that someone could use my pain to increase his private practice. After a short discussion, the group members asked him to leave. We wanted to be together with people who were living the pain, not studying it.

"I spent my whole life in the shadow of my brother's manic depression. Everything centered around his mood swings, his hospitalizations, his sickness. Because I was the 'healthy' child in the family, my parents left me alone to my own devices. This conference reminded me once again that my problems were secondary to my brother's illness. It's pretty hard to compete with something as dramatic as suicide. I hope the medical establishment gets it through its head that there are lots of us who are affected by suicide and we also need help. It's like we're the forgotten victims."

During any crisis, it is often difficult to admit that we need outside guidance to assist us in working out our problems. For many survivors, this reluctance to seek help is often intensified by the belief that conventional support systems failed in preventing the suicide of a family member.

"I was so disillusioned by how my wife was treated that going to a psychiatrist after her suicide was the last thing on my mind," explains Saul, a seventy-eight-year-old former businessman who lives in a retirement village in Florida. "My wife suffered from long-term depression, which no treatment or medication seemed to alleviate. One Friday night, twelve years ago, she was having a particularly bad episode. She turned to me, saying that she thought she should be hospitalized. I called her doctor, who said that it would be difficult to get her admitted over the weekend and she should come see him on Monday. That night, she took a whole bunch of different pills. When I woke up in the morning, she was dead beside me in the bed.

"I believe that my wife was written off because of her long history of suicide attempts. At the very least, the doctor could have told me to take her to the emergency room. The greatest myth is that if people talk about suicide or if they have had several unsuccessful attempts, they're not going to do it. Of course they are. I'm not saying that if my wife had survived that weekend she would not have killed herself eventually, but she was desperately asking for help and she didn't get it.

"During her funeral, I found great comfort from the rituals and prayers. I was never a very religious person but I started going to church every Sunday after my wife's death. The minister was very sympathetic, as were the other parishioners. I never felt they held me accountable for the suicide; just the opposite—there was a wonderful outpouring of support. My spiritual faith has helped me accept the mystery of her illness and her decision to end her life."

Coming to terms with the suicide of a loved one is confusing enough for an adult; for children, the loss is complicated by parents or others trying to explain the dual concepts of death, then death by choice.

"When my daughter was two, she asked me if she had a daddy," says Carol, the Minneapolis magazine publisher whose husband drowned himself when she was nine months pregnant. "She had just started going to play groups, where she could see that other children had fathers. I answered no, that her daddy had died. She began repeating the phrase over and over, 'My daddy died,' singing and chanting it. Obviously, she had no idea what it meant. Then, when she was three, she began showing her father's photograph to everyone who came to the house, explaining that her daddy was not at home because he was dead.

"There had been other deaths in my family since my daughter was born—a cousin died of AIDS and an uncle of a stroke—and eventually she asked me how her daddy had died. She loves to swim and I didn't want her to be afraid of the water. How could I tell her that her father had drowned himself? Initially, I sought advice from a child psychiatrist who, unfortunately, had absolutely no insight into the phenomenon of suicide. If you ask me, she seemed very uncomfortable with the topic. She told me I should tell my daughter that her father had suffered from a mental illness. To me, this seemed awfully heavy for a young child to absorb.

"My own therapist then recommended a psychologist who was a suicide survivor himself. He was absolutely wonderful. He explained to me that I should never lie to my daughter but that I didn't have to tell her all the details about her father's death in chronological sequence. I owned the story, he emphasized, and should shape my responses as her ability to assimilate the facts matured.

"She now understands that her daddy died while he was swimming because he was not feeling well and became tired. As she gets older, I'm sure she'll ask more questions and I will try to be as honest with her as I can. I will not make anything up; I will just cushion my description accordingly. In any case, I have to accept that her father's suicide will deeply affect her life in one way or the other. Last month, we were at the community center where she takes her swimming lessons. After finishing her laps, she got out of the pool and came over to me. She wanted to continue swimming but thought she should use a life jacket. When I asked her why, she said she was feeling a bit tired. I was so sad as I watched my daughter swim back and forth in her little orange jacket. Who knows what she was thinking? Yet, I feel it's in her best interest if I am honest with her. If she has one constant in her life, it will be that she will always be able to trust me."

Some children who are brought up on half-truths or outright lies regarding the suicide of a family member try to reconstruct the specifics of what happened by making contact with their relative's therapist. "I understood that if I didn't achieve some kind of closure about my mother's suicide, I would also self-destruct," explains Phil, a college student at a large Midwestern university. "When I was ten, I came home from school to find my mother dead on the living room sofa. There was an empty bottle of sleeping pills near her but no note. My mom had been very sad since my little brother was born. She told me she was seeing a doctor to make her happy again but I knew something was wrong with her.

"My father wouldn't talk to me about her suicide. Forget about sending me to therapy: He would rant and rave at psychiatrists, calling them witch doctors or rip-off artists. One year later, my father remarried and sold our house. It was as if my mother had never even existed. I got along with my stepmother and we all seemed to be okay. But in my senior year of high school, I began to get heavy into drugs. By the time I was in college, I was snorting cocaine on a daily basis.

"My girlfriend kept begging me to stop, telling me I was going to kill myself one day. On some level, I knew my behavior had to do with my mom's suicide. I promised my girlfriend I would see the drug counselor at school. He basically saved my life. It was his suggestion that I try to find my mother's doctor in order to begin to put her death to rest.

"My aunt gave me the name of the psychiatrist who had been treating my mother. I was surprised at his openness with me. He took out my mother's records and explained that she was suffering from postpartum depression. He also gave me some articles to read on the subject. Then he told me how much my mom had loved me, how she talked about me all the time and was very proud of me. I could see that he felt very bad about her death, like he had failed her. Yet, for some reason, I didn't blame him. He wasn't defensive, just sad. I went to see him a couple of times. Talking to him made me feel more connected to my mother, less alone. Reality might be more painful than numbing-out on drugs, but it's easier to deal with than secrets and lies."

Like Phil, many survivors seek support as part of an instinctive desire not to be pulled down by the tragedy and senselessness of their loss. "The more obsessed I became about my brother's suicide, the more I knew I needed help," says Betsy, a forty-two-year-old housewife from a small town in Oklahoma. "My brother shot himself four years ago, leaving behind three small children. After his death, I thought I had lost my mind. For the first couple of months, I couldn't think of anything else, even neglecting my own family as a result. Finally, I called a local mental health organization to see where I could get help. The only places they had listed were for people who wanted to kill themselves. Obviously, they were of no use to me.

"I then decided to research the subject of suicide at the library. There was an article written by a professor at the state university. I looked up his telephone number in the directory and called him up cold. I just blurted out what my brother had done, adding that I was at the end of my rope. It was the most painful thing I have ever done in my life—not only asking for help, but asking for help from a total stranger.

"I will never forget that man as long as I live. He talked to me on the phone for more than an hour. He reassured me that my feelings were normal, that I was not crazy. He gave me information on suicide support groups in my area and told me to call him whenever I felt like it. The nearest group was two hours from my home but I didn't care. I drove there the first Wednesday of every month for almost three years, and those meetings were my lifeline. I found incredible power from listening to all the different stories. It's much easier to forgive other people—you hear their stories and you know it's not their fault. Then you ask, 'Why should I be so hard on myself?' Gradually, my guilt over my brother's death began to recede. I can honestly say that I cared for each and every person in that group. I pray that they're all well."

Like Betsy, I, too, feel a permanent bond to all the people I have met in suicide support groups. Some of them have become my closest friends; others I will never see again. But their stories remain with me, their courage inspires me when waves of regret and sadness about my husband's suicide unexpectedly wash over me.

Presently, I attend support groups once or twice a year, usually near the anniversary of Harry's death. It is a difficult time of year, falling between Thanksgiving and Christmas, and the groups are usually quite full. As always, within minutes of going around the circle, I am as connected to these former strangers as I am to my own family.

At the last meeting I attended, a woman spoke whose husband had recently shot himself after a long and, what she considered to be, happy marriage. I recognized my earlier self sitting before me. Seven years ago I had sat in the same room, with the same look of numb disbelief and dazed bewilderment. Yet, now when I told the group my story, I could sense a distancing of emotion that only time can create. After the meeting ended, several people came up to me to thank me for my words. I went over to the woman who had lost her husband. She was pulling on her coat, as if on automatic pilot.

"I'm so sorry for your loss," I told her. "But it will get better." I reached out to hug her and she embraced me like a drowning person. We cried together, grieving for each other's pain and our own unique anguish. I knew her more intimately than most people in my life. I also knew—even if she did not—that she would heal. I remembered seeing Hal from the bus only months before. He had wanted desperately to get on with his life. With the flow of time he—and the rest of us—were able to do so. For survivors, help comes in many forms. Every one of them reassures us that we are not alone.

13

The Public Suicide

"Death by suicide is usually considered a newsworthy event. Perhaps it is because the person who chooses to respond to life's vicissitudes in this way challenges our usual attitudes toward life."

—Karen Dunne-Maxim,
Suicide and Its Aftermath: Understanding and Counseling the Survivors

I am waiting at the supermarket checkout line when I feel my heart skip a beat. Facing me on the magazine display rack is a copy of *New York* magazine with a large white cat gazing upward and the splashing headline: IS YOUR CAT CONTEMPLATING SUICIDE? Oh, no, I think to myself. Now it's even news when your *pet* dies? The article turns out to be about neurotic animals in New York City. Yet, the marketing people are on to something: Suicide sells.

Self-inflicted death both fascinates and repels. It is a mystery that can never be solved, a forbidden boundary that has defiantly been crossed. Rock stars, poets, politicians, police officers, millionaires—their suicides tap into the dark side of our personal and public psyche, reminding us of the fragile margin between the will to survive and the ultimate forsaking of hope.

The suicide of Vincent Foster, President Clinton's close friend and former aide, touched a particularly raw nerve among those who have trouble accepting a person's premeditated decision to die. Despite conclusive police evidence establishing that Mr. Foster committed suicide, congressional committees and members of the media continue to question the circumstances surrounding his death. Suggestions of a cover-up, ranging from accusations that his suicide note was forged to the alleged sighting of a mysterious assassin, have been offered as proof that Mr. Foster died against his will.

According to Karen Dunne-Maxim, the public's reaction to celebrity suicides often mirrors the denial found in many families following the suicide of one of its members.

"In working with suicide families, one often finds that there is conflict among family members about the real cause of death," she writes in *Suicide and Its Aftermath: Understanding and Counseling the Survivors*. "Sometimes even in the face of overwhelming evidence to the contrary (there may be a history of depression, psychiatric treatment and previous suicide attempts), some family members cling to the notion that the death was accidental or caused by foul play. This conflict is apparent in the controversy about the very public death of Marilyn Monroe. Many years later, the media is still used to express the opinion of those who feel the death was most certainly a suicide and by others who continue to search for the evidence that it was murder. This pattern so closely resembles what one observes in families after a suicide that one wonders if the *public family* is experiencing the same discordance over the suicide and ultimate rejection by this much idolized film star."

The suicide of a prominent member of society exposes the myth that material and professional success ensures happiness and well-being. The noted American poet Edwin Arlington Robinson captured the disbelief of a small town at the suicide of one of its most prominent and envied citizens in "Richard Corey," written in 1897:

> Whenever Richard Corey went down town
> We people on the pavement looked at him:
> He was a gentleman from sole to crown,
> Clean favored, and imperially slim.
>
> And he was always quietly arrayed,
> And he was always human when he talked;
> But still he fluttered pulses when he said,
> 'Good-morning,' and he glittered when he walked.
>
> And he was rich—yes, richer than a king—
> And admirably schooled in every grace:
> In fine, we thought that he was everything
> To make us wish that we were in his place.
>
> So on we worked, and waited for the light,
> And went without the meat, and cursed the bread;
> And Richard Corey, one calm summer night,
> Went home and put a bullet through his head.

Even more disquieting is the decision of a person to commit suicide despite having emerged triumphant from past suffering and pain. We are shaken and confused when Lewis Puller, Jr., the author of *Fortunate Son*, who lost half his body in the Vietnam War, shoots himself in the basement of his house after serving as an inspiration in courage to an entire generation of veterans. We try to make sense of the death of Tadeusz Borowski, the noted Polish writer who survived the gas chambers of Auschwitz and Dachau, only to take his life five years later by turning on the gas valve in his apartment three days after the birth of his daughter. We look for meaning when the prominent Holocaust scholar Terrence Des Pres kills himself following the publication of his book *The Survivor*, which chronicles the nobility of the human spirit in the face of utter hopelessness and despair.

Public suicides are often portrayed as daringly heroic or romantically tragic. The press characterizes the death pact of a thirteen-year-old girl and a fourteen-year-old boy in Miami, who drowned together in a canal because her parents forbade the relationship, as a modern-day Romeo and Juliet story. Ernest Hemingway is lionized as a "real man" for having the courage to blow his brains out. The rock star Kurt Cobain becomes an instant icon after shooting himself in the head at the age of twenty-seven.

"One of the women in my college dorm was totally obsessed with Sylvia Plath," says Esther, a twenty-five-year-old medical student from North Carolina. "She would talk almost mystically about how this brilliant, artistic woman had killed herself at the age of thirty-one by putting her head in the oven while her two young children were sleeping in the next room. She seemed more interested in her suicide than in her actual poetry. The summer before we graduated, she took an overdose of tranquilizers at her parents' beach house. She left a copy of one of Sylvia Plath's poems on the night table beside the empty pill bottles. I guess the whole thing seemed so dramatic to her. It just seemed stupid to me—and sad, very sad."

Because a suicide is a murder with a known assailant but an indeterminate motive, its retelling is often accompanied by personal interpretation, conjecture, and a Rorschach-test set of individual responses. Press accounts frequently focus on sensational details and speculative theories, serving to compound the pain and surrealism of the ordeal for the survivor.

"The front page of the New York *Post* read LOVE SICK DOC IN SUICIDE LEAP," recalls Victoria, a stylish woman in her mid-forties whose husband, one of the most prominent heart surgeons in the country, jumped to his death from their thirteenth-floor Park Avenue apartment eight years ago. "The reporter spoke to one of my neighbors, who said I used to spend weekends in our country home in Connecticut with my children from my first marriage. She just assumed Rob and I were having problems and told the press that. I was in a total state of shock but the story made it through to my consciousness: They were blaming me for my husband's death because I had left him alone to spend time with my two young sons.

"My husband landed in the courtyard of the building, in full view of all the residents. It was ten o'clock on a Monday morning and the janitor was out there getting the trash. Rob's body fell next to him. I still feel guilty about that janitor and would tip him extra at Christmas, as if it were somehow my fault. The doorman also saw the body fall and called 911.

"Rob killed himself on the third anniversary of his mother's death. The doorman later told me that he had gone out at dawn, returning with a six-pack of beer. He never left for the hospital to make rounds, something he did every morning, seven days a week. I was still in Connecticut, getting ready to come to New York. I had gotten up early and thought about phoning him because I knew he would be sad about his mother. But then I just assumed he was in the operating room like he was every day at that time. I always wonder what would have happened if I had made that call. I can't believe that while he was jumping out the window, I was in the shower thinking about what to make for that night's dinner.

"The police telephoned me in Connecticut, advising me not to come home because they had to seal off the apartment to search for evidence. It took them eight hours to determine that his death was a suicide. His body lay in the courtyard the whole time, covered with a yellow tarpaulin that someone had thrown over him.

"The doorman eventually gave me all the details of what happened. He said that Rob's right hand had been severed, his head split open. He was wearing a white dress shirt, gray trousers, socks, and no shoes. Rob always used to wear shoes in the house, and I later found them on the floor near the jump window.

"The news about my husband's suicide appeared on television around one in the afternoon. The first report was on CNN—'Prominent Park Avenue heart surgeon falls to his death.' I started getting all these calls in Connecticut. Some were from people in the building, screaming at me to get the body out of the courtyard before their kids came home from school. My mother saw the broadcast in Florida and called me, hysterical. I was numb. I couldn't believe that I was not also dead. I thought that the inside of me had died. Why was the outside of me moving when the inside of me was dead? It was impossible to believe that I could still be alive.

"I had to go to the city the next day to identify the body at the medical examiner's office. There were reporters in front of the building, people were taking my picture. It seemed all part of one big dream. It felt as if I had to climb thousands of stairs to get into the front door; it was like going up a giant mountain. Two friends came with me. Back then, they made you look at the actual body instead of photographs like they do now. We were taken to an area that I thought was a holding room. I assumed someone would come greet us, because my husband was famous and there was a lot of press interest in his death.

"We were standing there for around ten minutes when I heard the sound of wheels on marble floors. All of a sudden, the doors to the room flew open and two people entered, rolling in a gurney with a body on it. It was wrapped from head to toe in a white sheet. They pulled the sheet off and it was Rob. He was totally exposed, even his genitalia. His bones were protruding from his body, his mouth and eyes were open, and he was covered with blood.

"I had no idea that they were going to show me the whole body. I imagined that it would be like the movies, where they pull out a shelf from the wall and you just look at the person's face and say, 'Yes, that's him.' I was standing in front of Rob's missing right hand, his operating hand. I screamed, 'Oh my God,' and then I fainted. When I came to, my friends helped lead me out of the room.

"It took me five thousand dollars and six weeks to get a court order so I could enter my apartment. All this time, reporters were trying to get to me, to find out the 'real' reason why Rob had killed himself. There were several stories implying that he had a drinking problem. Even though I knew he was a fine surgeon, I felt at a loss to safeguard his reputation. First I had failed him as his wife; now I was failing him as his widow.

"I went into a terrible depression after my husband died. Even though people were shocked, I continued living in the apartment until just a year ago. There was a horrible feeling there, that was true. But it was all I had left. I could pour myself a glass of wine, put on the music, and think for one split second that maybe it didn't happen. The feeling that my old world was intact, even for an instant, was worth it, worth living there."

The public nature of suicide results in unsolicited commentary and instant analysis, infringing on a survivor's intimate pain and introspection. "There is a total loss of privacy," says Mark, a fifty-six-year-old mechanical engineer from Tennessee whose wife jumped from the roof of a Nashville office building in the middle of rush hour. "The newspapers wrote that my wife had recently been laid off from her job and was under treatment for depression. They also ran a picture of her body lying in the middle of the street. Her skirt was up around her neck and you could see her underpants. My wife's anguish was splayed out for the world to see. All her dignity had been taken away, making her death even harder to accept."

Some survivors try to hide the truth that their loved ones have killed themselves, only to see the details of their suicides recounted in the media. "I told everyone that my son had shot himself while playing Russian roulette," says Nick, a forty-seven-year-old accountant from Rhode Island. "I had no idea the local paper would care enough about a sixteen-year-old boy to run a front-page story saying the coroner had ruled his death a suicide, not an accident. I had lied to everyone and now the whole world could see I had been unable to protect my own son.

"The article described how my son had shot himself with my pistol, quoted from his suicide note, and mentioned that he had recently had a minor mishap with the law. In addition, the reporter spoke to an expert in the field of teenage suicide, who advised parents to get professional help for their children if they seemed depressed and to avoid keeping guns in the house. How do you think that made me feel? It's been almost a year but I'm thinking of selling my home and moving away. The whole town knows my business and it seems as if there's no place to hide."

Parents who have lost their teenage children to self-inflicted gunshot wounds often experience an intensified sense of responsibility because of the well-documented connection between the ready availability of firearms and suicide. According to the Centers for Disease Control and Prevention, people living in a household where a firearm is kept are nearly five times more likely to die by suicide than people who live in gun-free homes. *The New England Journal of Medicine* reports that the rate of suicide by firearms among adolescents and young people has more than doubled over the past twenty-five years, and warns: "Owners of firearms should weigh their reasons for keeping a gun in the home against the possibility that it might someday be used in a suicide."

The Centers for Disease Control and Prevention also report that in the United States more people kill themselves with guns than by all other methods combined. Suicide by firearms accounts for 61 percent of all suicides, followed by hanging and strangulation (14.5 percent), gas poisoning (7.5 percent), other poisoning (10 percent), and other causes (7 percent). Nearly 80 percent of all firearm suicides are committed by white men, who account for 73 percent of all suicides in the country.

The phenomenon of murder-suicide, when a person commits homicide and shortly after commits suicide, accounts for one thousand to fifteen hundred combined suicide and homicide deaths in the United States each year. The *Journal of the American Medical Association* points out that while suicide occurs among men and women across all ages, murder-suicide is committed principally by young males with intense sexual jealousy, depressed mothers, or despairing elderly men with ailing wives. The principal victims of murder-suicide are female sexual partners or blood relatives, usually young children.

"I sometimes think, murder is murder: What's the difference between killing another person or killing yourself?" says Mary, a thirty-seven-year-old St. Louis mother of three young children whose husband, a television anchorman, shot himself two years ago. "Gil's suicide was covered as if it were the crime of the century. For one week, story after story speculated as to why he had ended his life in the prime of a successful career. One article even mentioned that Gil might have been depressed because our daughter suffers from cerebral palsy. I was used to my husband's reporting the news, not being the focus of it. But his death was a hot story, there was nothing I could do about it.

"The night Gil killed himself, we had people over for dinner. He said I should go to sleep, that he would clean up. When the police called to tell me that Gil was dead, I remember looking at the sun coming up through the red curtains in our bedroom. The cops said he had shot himself in his office. I figured I was dreaming, that everything would be back to normal when I woke up. Then I heard my baby crying. Even though my husband was dead, my son still needed his morning bottle. Life was not stopping because Gil was no longer here.

"The reporters kept asking me if I had found a note. It seemed so important to them, as if it would unravel the riddle of Gil's death. Two weeks after the funeral, I opened the drawer where I keep all my bills. I saw this ripped-up yellow legal paper with my husband's handwriting on it compressed into a ball. At that moment, I thought I was having an out-of-body experience. I started searching frantically for something to piece the scraps of paper together but all I could find was thick black electrical tape—it made the note look even crazier than it was.

"I could barely understand what Gil had written. His words made no sense, something about loving me but having run out of choices. I called the police and they came over immediately. I didn't know they would take the note away; if I had, I wouldn't have given it to them. They didn't even give me a photocopy. One of the reporters must have had a source in the police department because the next day there was a photograph of the note in the newspaper, electrical tape and all.

"After the initial press interest, Gil's death was basically forgotten. People seem more interested in figuring out the reason for suicide, the logic of self-destruction, than in its consequences. Now, I only confront the truth in dark little corners. I obsess about Gil's note, aching for the chance to convince him that he did have choices, that we could have worked something out. I take long showers, put the stereo on very loud, and cry. I do this to protect my children, so they won't know the depth of my confusion and hurt."

Suicide notes are written by approximately 25 percent of people who kill themselves, according to John McIntosh in *Suicide and Its Aftermath: Understanding and Counseling the Survivors.* Yet, like Mary, many survivors find these last messages from their loved ones to be more confusing than comforting. Because the notes are often composed during states of extreme agitation, their incoherent references and cryptic allusions usually bring about more uncertainty than resolution.

I searched for days for a note from Harry. Seven years after his suicide, there is still a part of me that hopes—and fears—that one day I will open one of his books or come across a forgotten audiotape that will contain his thoughts as he faced the last hours of his life. I, too, like the public and the press, crave a tidy explanation to the unfathomable act of choosing death over life. I would like nothing more than to have a sound-bite answer ready for the inevitable question of why my husband committed suicide, a one-sentence *because* that would serve as reassuring balm.

After Vincent Foster killed himself, *The Wall Street Journal* ran an editorial declaring, "The American public is entitled to know if Mr. Foster's death was somehow connected to his high office. If he was driven to take his life by purely personal despair, a serious investigation should share this conclusion so that he can be *appropriately mourned.*" (Emphasis added.)

Unfortunately, the newspaper fails to comprehend what survivors have come to accept: The torturous ambiguity that suicide leaves as its legacy allows no room for definitive closure or "appropriate" mourning. The challenge of surviving is to mourn without understanding; with pain and grief, yes, but with the awareness that we will never know why we have been left by those we have loved.

Long-term
Effects

*"Not all survivors are affected in the same fashion
or to the same degree."*

—John McIntosh,
*Suicide and Its Aftermath: Understanding and Counseling
the Suicide Survivor*

Nothing prepares you for the first anniversary. I steel myself
for weeks beforehand, warned by other survivors to fasten
my seat belt for the rough ride ahead. I trust that my custom-
ary neutral regard for special occasions such as birthdays and
holidays will somehow insulate me. I make plans to busy myself. I attend extra support groups. But like a tornado striking
its target with exact precision, as December 16 approaches,
the minute-to-minute, hour-to-hour, day-to-day recollections

of my husband's suicide engulf me, temporarily blowing down whatever stability I think I have achieved over the past year.

By the second anniversary, my protective numbness burns off, propelling the details of Harry's suicide to the surface with exquisite sharpness. Yet, I decide it is finally time for me to look at his photograph. I pull out the last of the many albums Harry and I had accumulated during our twenty-one-year marriage, selecting the most recent picture of him I can find. I look in his eyes to see if I can discover the turmoil. But he looks happy, smiling at our muddy dog emerging from the lake in Central Park. When did Harry start thinking of death? I begin to anguish. How could I have missed it? I quickly shut the album, ambushed by a grief as raw as the day he died.

Each year, I believe myself to be inured against the pain; I will it. Yet, now, as the seventh anniversary of Harry's suicide nears, I am again transported to that time of horror and chaos, of total disbelief and utter madness. I am filled with unremitting regret: What a waste, I say to myself over and over, obsessively repeating a mantra that offers no comfort. Harry has missed so much over the years. I've grown older while he has remained young. And, of course, the *why*. The never-to-be-solved riddle of another person's private desperation. I know instinctively that even as I move on, as my life falls into place without him, the effects of Harry's decision to kill himself will be with me always.

According to John McIntosh in *Suicide and Its Aftermath: Understanding and Counseling the Suicide Survivor*, suicide survivors share many of the same psychological reactions as people who have experienced traumatic events such as rape, war, and crime victimization. The mental health community now recognizes that suicide survivors can suffer post-traumatic stress disorder, defined by the American Psychiatric Association as "the development of characteristic symptoms following a psychologically traumatic event that is generally outside the range of human experience."

The initial symptoms of post-traumatic stress disorder include "physic numbing," or "emotional anesthesia," where one is unable to recall important aspects of the traumatic event. This is followed by feelings of detachment or estrangement from other people, a loss of interest in previously enjoyed activities, and an inability to feel emotions of any type, especially those associated with intimacy, tenderness, and sexuality. There are also difficulties in falling or staying asleep, nightmares, an inability to concentrate or complete tasks, and a fear of losing control. Long-term effects include intense psychological distress when exposed to events that resemble an aspect of the event, especially the anniversary of the trauma.

"I tried having a picnic on the first anniversary of my sister's death but I couldn't carry it off," says Pam, a thirty-seven-year-old social worker from Springfield, Illinois, whose sister killed herself two years ago after undergoing exhaustive chemotherapy for ovarian cancer. "Although I wanted the occasion to be a joyous celebration of Caroline's life, as the day got closer, I couldn't stop crying. I had no idea it would be that rough—I had never put great stock in anniversaries before, but this was different. I began having vivid recollections of the events that occurred before and after my sister's death, images I must have previously suppressed. It was as if I were finally watching a home video about Caroline's suicide without the jumble of static obstructing the reception.

"Caroline was a year older than me—we were practically twins. She had been completely devastated by the effects of her chemo; all her hair had fallen out and she was thin as a rail. She had lost all hope, knowing the odds of making it were against her. One night, when her husband was away on a business trip, she swallowed all the pills she had in the house, drank some alcohol, and turned on the gas in the kitchen. I called her the next morning before I went to work, like I did every day, and the minute her answering machine picked up, I knew something was wrong. I drove over to her house in a panic, figuring that she was unable to come to the phone because she had fallen or fainted. The possibility that she might have killed herself never entered my mind: At that time, suicide was a totally foreign concept to me.

"Weeks later, when I was going through her things, I found one of those books that tell you how to kill yourself. Caroline had underlined specific passages in yellow Magic Marker, following the step-by-step instructions on how to die to the letter. She had even lined up the bottles of pills and alcohol on her dresser, like the book advised, so the police would know it was a suicide, not a murder. As I looked through the death manual, my hands began to shake. Why couldn't Caroline have called me instead of listening to that garbage?

"The suicide feels very fresh, even after two years. I still have a hard time reading books or seeing television shows related to sisters. I find Caroline's birthday to be incredibly stressful, the same for Christmas. I also find myself having thoughts of suicide, even though I don't think they're for real. I had been so inspired by my sister's struggle to survive: What pushed her to finally give in to her despondency? My life feels on hold now, all my thoughts seem to revolve around suicide. I recently joined a survivor support group and people there assure me that it gets better—I pray that they are right."

Because of the traumatic nature of suicide, certain dates such as anniversaries, holidays, and birthdays take on greater significance for the survivor, observe Karen Dunne-Maxim, Edward Dunne, and Marilyn Hauser in *Suicide and Its Aftermath: Understanding and Counseling the Suicide Survivor.* "We have seen many families who dread the approach of these occasions as unwanted reminders of their pain. It is our belief that holidays and birthdays should be observed recognizing the loss but using new family rituals which promote both celebration and healing."

Dennis, a college junior from Indiana whose sixteen-year-old brother hanged himself ten months ago, describes the immense solace his family found from lighting a candle for his brother during Thanksgiving dinner. "The burning flame in front of what would have been Brad's place at the table made it seem as if he were still with us. Although there was this gaping hole in our family, it helped to acknowledge my brother's presence in whatever way we could. Brad was only a kid, a kid who killed himself after his basketball team lost an important game because he had nervously thrown the scoring shot for the wrong side. No one from my family had attended the game and we only found out what happened later. Even now, I don't think I have really quite processed his suicide. It's too difficult to think that my brother was so humiliated and ashamed, that he could have been hurting so intensely. On some level, I'm still waiting for him to come home. There's a part of me that wouldn't be surprised if the phone rang right now and it was Brad, going on about some football game he had just seen. I suppose the shock of his death is still too great for me to grasp."

Like Dennis, many survivors find it almost impossible to absorb the totality of losing a loved one to suicide. "After four years, there's a part of me that believes Max might really be alive," says Vera, a sixty-three-year-old trustee of several cultural and educational institutions in Pittsburgh. "My husband was a very successful businessman who started getting nervous that his company would go bankrupt. This was a very real fear because he had expanded during the 1980s and was now over-extended. Even though I tried to reassure him that things would work out—they always did—he became consumed with money fears. As Max became more overwhelmed financially, he started not being able to cope. He would come home from work earlier and earlier and would watch television or just look out the window. He even stopped reading, although it had been one of his greatest pleasures.

"As Max became more depressed, I felt myself pulling away from him. He refused to go for help, arguing that no shrink could solve his business problems, so what would be the use? As he was becoming more dependent on me to make all the decisions, he was also acting more combative, like a small child. The worse he got, the deeper I went into denial. Looking back at that time, I believe there was a certain inevitability to my husband's self-destruction. Three months before he died, he said to me that we should both consider killing ourselves. I answered that if we did that, the kids wouldn't get any life insurance. He responded, so uncharacteristically, 'Who cares?'

"The weekend before Max took his life, we went to our country house. On Monday, I returned to the city for a doctor's appointment while he stayed up there. As I was sitting in the doctor's office, I suddenly had this intense feeling of apprehension about my husband's safety. I asked the receptionist if I could use the phone to call him in the country, but there was no answer. I then left a message for him at our home and his office, just in case he had changed his mind and decided to come back to the city. By now, I was extremely agitated; I felt myself losing control. I left the doctor's office without seeing him, driving home at what seemed one hundred miles an hour.

"I knew in my gut that something was wrong. For several hours, I called the country house every twenty minutes, praying that Max would pick up. Finally, I phoned our next-door neighbor up there to ask him to check if Max was all right. After what seemed like an eternity, he called me back. As soon as he said, 'Are you alone?' I knew that Max was dead. I heard myself screaming, as if I were very far away. He said he had found Max dead in his car in the garage, with rags stuffed under the doors to keep the exhaust from escaping. 'You're a liar,' I screamed at him. 'That's a stranger in the car. Max would never do this to me.' I was hysterical.

"I somehow remember calling my daughter. She drove me up to the country house in a two-hour ride that seemed completely unreal. When we arrived, there were police all over the house. I ran over to them, shrieking that it was impossible the dead man was my husband. The house was a total mess because the police had ransacked it looking for evidence. We had a large collection of antique clocks and I noticed that they had all stopped. This fact struck me in the middle of the insanity.

"The police started questioning me, asking if my husband had enemies, if he had been sick, and other really intrusive questions. I couldn't believe they were talking about this when I was in such a state. I asked to see my husband, but they told me the coroner had already taken his body away. I was furious. 'This is private property,' I yelled. 'You can't take away my things.' Everything became such a blur after that; it was like a nightmare come true.

"Even though I saw Max at the funeral parlor, there was part of me that didn't believe it was him. He was such an exuberant man and this thing just lying there was not my husband. For months after his suicide, I suffered from paralyzing anxiety attacks and constant nightmares. My daughter entered a deep depression and my son stopped talking about his father. Four years later, my children will still not mention his name or anything about him, even at holidays or family gatherings. I find this very painful.

"Two years ago, one of Max's business acquaintances called me to say that he had just come back from Israel and was almost sure he had seen Max there. I immediately thought it was true, that my husband had not really died. Somebody had slipped another person's body into his car and Max was now in Israel under the witness protection program. I know I'm being irrational but ever since then, I have not been able to go to Israel. On the one hand, I'm scared I'll see him, and on the other hand, I'm scared I won't.

"The first year after Max died, I went to synagogue every Friday night to say Kaddish for him. I was never an observant person, but as I recited this ancient prayer for the dead, I found an unexpected comfort. There was an order in the rituals, a serenity in the prescribed traditions. I eventually joined the synagogue, not only for this sense of continuity but also for the feeling of community it gave me. I never imagined growing old without Max by my side; I still can't believe that he left me so violently. Yet, in order for me to move on, I must create a world that is both steady and constant. Only when I rebuild can I finally put my husband to rest. I must have the faith that I will be able to do this."

Even as we try to restore order to our lives, survivors find that we are often troubled by recurring images of sudden death and unforeseen disaster. "Ever since my cousin killed himself, I find myself waiting for something else to happen, for the other shoe to drop," says Polly, a forty-four-year-old tour guide from Hawaii. "Three years ago on Christmas Day, my cousin walked into the ocean and drowned himself. My son, who was twelve at the time, had been very close to him and took his death very hard. Now, I'm afraid for him. I sent him to a therapist, but after several sessions, he refused to continue. I'm really scared. What happens if my son gets depressed and also decides to kill himself?

"Suicide was always something that other people did; it never happened to 'normal' families like mine. Now I believe that anyone is capable of doing it. Recently, a friend came over for dinner and asked to use the bathroom to wash up. She was in there for what seemed a very long time and I became convinced that she must be killing herself. I started pounding frantically on the door, certain she was dead. My friend came running out of the bathroom, looking at me as if I were crazy. Obviously, suicide is never far from my mind. It happened once, and I keep waiting for it to happen again."

In addition to worrying that catastrophe will inevitably strike us once again, survivors are frequently overcome by powerful feelings of isolation and despair, especially as the anniversary of our loved one's suicide approaches. Other survivors, especially those who have lost a parent, find themselves experiencing extreme emotional distress as they near the age when their mother or father committed suicide, similar to the "anniversary reaction" experienced by some children of Holocaust survivors when they reach the age when their parent was taken away by the Nazis.

"I went into a terrible depression right after my forty-fifth birthday," recalls Gail, a fifty-four-year-old teacher from Vancouver. "Everything seemed hopeless. It took all my courage to just get out of bed in the morning. Life had no meaning— why should I even continue? I never even made the connection to my mother's suicide until I reluctantly entered therapy. During the first session, I mentioned that my mother had killed herself when I was fifteen. My therapist asked me how old my mother had been when she died, and I casually answered, forty-five. It was like being hit by lightning. I was reliving what I imagined my mother had been going through when she gave up and ended her life.

"My mother had a drinking problem ever since I could remember, and she died from mixing pills with alcohol. I initially fought the idea that her death was intentional, telling myself she had been too drunk to know what she was doing. Even when I found out that she had refilled the prescriptions for her pills on the day before she died, I still had a hard time accepting that she had really meant to kill herself. It was my way of not having to think of how unhappy she must have been.

"Because my mother and I were having terrible fights for months before she died, I believed her death was her way of getting back at me. You know, like when you're little and you're mad at your parents—you imagine how they would feel when you die and how they would cry at your funeral. That's what I thought she had done. At the same time, I was also very relieved that she was dead. Her drinking had gotten steadily worse and I was afraid she would turn violent. I felt very guilty at being so relieved—I still do.

"I know now that I will never have any definite closure about my mother's suicide. Her death has entirely shaped my life, and the only way I can move on is to accept her decision, not be destroyed by it. I'll always be angry—and confused—that she chose to leave me in such a hurtful manner. But I have no more time to lose."

Like Gail, many survivors seek out professional guidance to help sort through the consequences of losing a loved one to suicide. But how does a therapist feel when one of his or her patients commits suicide? According to Dr. Frank Jones, Jr., a New Jersey psychiatrist who established one of the first survivor support groups for therapists, the suicide of a patient in therapy is the most difficult bereavement crisis a therapist will ever have to encounter and endure. "The situation is compounded because it presents not only a *personal* crisis, similar to that experienced by family members and others intimately involved with the decedent, but also a *professional* crisis related to a therapist's special role in society," he writes in *Suicide and Its Aftermath: Understanding and Counseling the Suicide Survivor.*

A survey of randomly selected psychotherapists in the United States conducted in 1986 revealed that 38.2 percent of the respondents had experienced the suicide of a patient. "Working through this loss is difficult," explains M. Gorkin in the *Bulletin of the Menninger Clinic,* "because the therapist cannot expect to arrive at an absolute conviction about *whether* and, if so, *when* he erred."

For a patient to lose a therapist to suicide can be equally devastating. "It is clear that when a therapist takes his or her own life we can anticipate clients' short-term reactions to be of great intensity, including increased risk of suicide," observes Edward Dunne in *Suicide and Its Aftermath: Understanding and Counseling the Suicide Survivor.* "We can also anticipate long-range reactions that may seriously impede functioning and possibly close off the patient's accessibility to help from the therapeutic community."

Wayne is a fifty-one-year-old business executive from San Francisco whose psychiatrist killed himself last year. "When I was laid off from my last job, I found myself at loose ends and decided to seek out counseling," he says. "It was a very big step for me to admit that something was wrong, but I knew I needed help to get back some control in my life. My doctor was wonderful, practical yet empathetic. One day, after seeing him once a week for almost seven months, I got a call from his secretary telling me that he had died. I was shocked: He was a relatively young man and seemed in fairly good health. When I asked his secretary what happened, she started crying. She said he had jumped off the Golden Gate Bridge on Sunday, just before dawn.

"To be honest, my reaction was totally selfish. How could this man who was supposedly encouraging me to face my problems just get up and leave? And what was he trying to tell me by committing suicide: that life wasn't worth it, so we should all just go jump off a bridge? His secretary offered to give me names of other psychiatrists so I could continue treatment. Forget it—there was no way I was going to expose myself to that again. Three months after my doctor killed himself, I was hired for a top management job at a leading pharmaceutical company. I then realized that even though my doctor had his own problems, the reality was that he had helped me regain much of the self-confidence I had lost when I was fired. Even though he must have been suffering, he did help me in many ways. I'm not angry now, just sorry at the death of such a good man. I guess we're all human, after all."

Regardless of our relationship to the person who chooses to commit suicide, the first step in the survivors' journey of healing is the recognition that this final and irrevocable act will forever reverberate throughout every aspect of our lives. Yet, as time goes by, the crushing grip of our loved one's decision eventually starts to ease, allowing us to honor his or her memory with even greater clarity.

"Each year, I find myself both more resigned and more at peace about my father's suicide," says Fran, a forty-seven-year-old nurse from a Chicago suburb. "But my mother still doesn't admit that my father killed himself, even after eight years. She continues to insist that he was cleaning his gun and it misfired. At the beginning, I also tried to convince myself his death was accidental. But I can't pretend anymore, not to myself and not to others. I have finally let air into my world, which was once sealed with secrets and lies. I feel I am giving my father the respect he deserves by acknowledging that his death is part of his life.

"After you called me, I told my mother I was going to be interviewed for a book about people who have survived the suicide of a loved one. She seemed surprised, asking me who we knew who had killed themselves. In the past, I would have said to her, 'Your husband, for God's sake. My father.' But now I let my mother be. We're all affected in different ways and we have to get through this the best way we can. It's hard enough being judged by others without judging ourselves."

With the passage of each anniversary of my husband's suicide, I am overcome by the irreversibility and irrationality of his loss. Yet, now my mourning is colored and affected by the changes that have occurred in my own life during this inevitable passage of time. The gradual diminishing in the intensity of my grief stirs the promise of unexpected possibilities, of unknown options. Although this feeling of hope is mixed with an inescapable sorrow, it is hope, nonetheless. Tentatively, I embrace it, and welcome it home.

Forgiving Them/
Forgiving Ourselves

> "Suicide sensitizes all of us to the extreme precariousness
> and preciousness of life, urging us to cherish and savor
> the life that we have, the relationships we enjoy, as
> much as we can for as long as we can."
>
> —Charles Rubey and David Clark,
> *Suicide and Its Aftermath: Understanding and Counseling the Survivors*

Several hours after I found Harry's body in his office, I called his best friend, Eduardo, with the news. The telephone connection to Bogotá, Colombia, was clear, and I could hear Eduardo's shocked gasp as distinctly as if he were standing next to me. "I am so sorry for you, Carla," he said immediately, catching his breath. "How are you doing?"

I was taken aback by his question. Eduardo, who had known Harry since they were in kindergarten together, was asking about *me*. Not why Harry had killed himself, not about the events preceding his suicide, not even the details concerning his death. But about my state of mind, how I was holding up. His concern touched deep within me, connecting to that part of me which somehow recognized that despite the chaos, I was still alive.

"People are going to say a lot of things to you," Eduardo continued. "Remember how much you and Harry loved each other. Then, turn around and walk away."

Eduardo's advice stayed with me during those first difficult months and years following Harry's death, guiding me like radar through a storm in which I was flying blind. Intuitively, I was aware that I could not allow myself to be thrown off course by the potentially dangerous turbulence created by the stigma and shame associated with suicide. In order to reach my destination, safely and intact, I knew I had to absolve my husband and myself for what each of us had done—or what each of us had failed to do.

"Grief is an unfolding process," says Rosemarie, the photographer from Boston whose mother jumped to her death from her bedroom window when Rosemarie was nineteen years old. "After so many years, I now feel strong enough to forgive my mother for taking her life. By accepting that her death is an integral part of who I am, I feel a greater sense of continuity and calmness. Recently, I framed some of the beautiful landscapes my mother had painted during one of her hospital stays and hung them up in my apartment. The pictures remind me that there was a creative force in her despair; that my mother's gifts did not die beside her on the gray sidewalk outside our home."

Like Rosemarie, I gradually began to incorporate the act of suicide as a choice my husband had made about his own life. Five years after I cleaned up the deathly clutter of his examining room, I sat in the solemn quiet of a legal conference room knowing that the sale of Harry's medical office would release me from far more than my legal and financial obligations. With the return of order, I could now afford the luxury of forgiveness. Although I was afraid that I would confuse forgiving with forgetting, I realized I must reclaim my life both to move on and to allow Harry to rest in peace.

"Accepting the death sometimes feels as if you are giving up the fight," says Valerie, a fifty-two-year-old lawyer from Virginia whose daughter killed herself ten years ago in her freshman year of college. "Forgiveness comes with resignation—after all, how many choices are there after this? Even though there is a release in surrendering, it comes with a price. You have to acknowledge your helplessness, that you cannot change the situation no matter what you do. I wanted desperately to stop time. Yet, the only way I could start living again was to give up trying to resurrect my daughter. I had to freeze her in my memory as she was *before* the suicide, before she actually left me.

"Kim was eighteen when she hanged herself in her college dorm room, the day after we had a terrible quarrel on the telephone. Her roommate called me at my office to tell me what happened and I screamed, 'It's not true.' I experienced the most excruciating pain I have ever felt in my life—it was as if my scalp were being ripped from my head.

"My husband, who prides himself on being a man of action, was as frozen as I. On the drive up to the college, we didn't say a word to each other. I had the sensation that I was melting into the seat, that time was passing so slowly but moving so fast at the same time. I really didn't believe that Kim was dead; it was my fantasy that as soon as we got to the college, everything would be okay. Yet, as each minute ticked away, I was convinced that I was losing any chance to save her.

"I never thought the pain would end. I cried for what seemed an eternity, afraid to stop because I didn't know what the next moment would bring. My own suicide seemed to be waiting in the wings. On some level, I understood that if I didn't move into another stage of grieving, ending my life would be the ultimate and inevitable outcome.

"The process of healing is like coming out of a coma. It took me several years to begin to appreciate the beauty of life once again. Yet, the more I saw I could enjoy myself, the more frightened I became that I was losing Kim. How could I take pleasure from a beautiful sunset or the ocean breeze in my hair when my daughter would never be able to do so? The pain of her loss dampened whatever flashes of optimism were starting to emerge.

"Eventually, I stopped trying to find the answer to why Kim had died. Now I no longer debate the whys in my head, the could-haves, the should-haves, the what-ifs. With suicide, the search for understanding is totally encompassing—there's no room for anything else. You have to give up the search in order to go forward. Ten years later, the question of why my daughter killed herself is more nostalgic than anything; it's no longer even rhetorical, just reminiscent of what seems like another lifetime. I try to remember that old pain but I can't imagine it anymore. The loss is the loss, whatever I do.

"It's almost scary to regain even the smallest part of who you were. I didn't triumph over the suicide, because if I did, I would have changed the outcome. I am never going to be the same person I was before Kim's death: I will always live with feelings of tremendous sadness and regret. Yet, at the same time, I find myself also experiencing moments of real happiness and feelings of hope for the future. Sorrow always parallels the joy. The sorrow is for them; the joy is for us. I believe that when these two emotions can coexist, forgiveness will follow."

For many survivors, acknowledging the deep anger we feel at being rejected by our loved one helps free us to move on. "It took me a long time to convince myself that my brother's suicide was not caused by whatever personal inadequacies I might have," says Walter, a retired businessman in his early seventies who lives in Phoenix, Arizona. "I was always the person who was most responsible for him. When Sid killed himself four years ago at the age of sixty-three, I had no doubt that I was to blame for his death. I had supported him financially for most of his life and helped him get on his feet every time he fell. Any time something was wrong, he would call me. Yet, this time—the most important time—he somehow decided he could not turn to me. I'll never know why.

"My brother suffered a nervous breakdown when he was in his teens, right after the death of our mother. I remember visiting him in the hospital. We went for a walk and Sid jumped into the road. I pulled him back but he said that he wanted to get hit by a car, that he didn't want to live anymore. I became very angry at him because I thought he was grandstanding. He was always the extrovert and I was the introvert. But now he seemed like a different person.

"My brother was in and out of psychiatric facilities his whole life. He would get better, stop taking his antidepressant medication, then get worse again. It was a cycle that repeated itself over and over. Even though he was never really happy, I couldn't believe that he would ever take his life. One day, I got a call from the police saying they had found his body in the parking lot of a local hospital, surrounded by several empty pill bottles. I was enraged. I had done everything in my power to keep my brother alive ever since we were boys, and now he had excluded me as if I were some kind of stranger. All the energy I had spent over the years to keep him alive didn't seem to matter. He never even gave me the chance to try to help him.

"I was furious after Sid died. In a way, the anger helped me cope with his absence. On the third anniversary of my brother's death, I was standing in front of his grave when I suddenly remembered the line 'It is a far, far better thing I do . . .' from *A Tale of Two Cities* by Charles Dickens. Well, maybe my brother's suicide was his way of saying, 'It is a far, far better place I go.' Sid wanted to leave this world and he did. This makes me very upset, but since I can't bring my brother back, I have no other option than to accept the manner in which he died."

As survivors come to relinquish, however reluctantly, the distinctly human conceit that we can change the people we care about and keep them alive through our love, we also find ourselves beginning to understand the true, solitary nature of death. "Even though suicide seems inconceivable and absurd, it is as real as you get," says Todd, a twenty-eight-year-old sales representative from Michigan whose father killed himself seven years ago. "I'm frightened at the idea that taking one's life can be considered rational because that implies a certain amount of logic to self-murder. If suicide is irrational, then it's just madness and there's a kind of closure. But if suicide is not crazy, then why should the rest of us continue to hold on when life, as it will at times, becomes unbearable?

"When my father shot himself, he took a free fall out of the scene. That instant, I grew up. Although I know I should forgive him because he did it to himself and not to me, I still believe—and probably will always believe—that if I had been a better son, he would not have died. Other parents hang on for their kids. Why not him? Most of the time, however, I try to forgive myself, not because I necessarily deserve it but because I want to get on with my life. What would it serve to brood and become depressed? I'm resigned now; I wasn't for a long time. Guilt will only pull me down and I don't want to end up in the ground beside my father.

"I've noticed that my values and activities have changed over the past years. Now my top priority is breathing out and breathing in—surviving. I have also found it important to connect with other people. I recently joined a suicide prevention organization in my area that runs a twenty-four-hour hotline and I'm training to be a volunteer to answer phone calls. I know I couldn't stop my father from killing himself, but maybe if I am able to prevent others from doing the same thing, his death will begin to make a little more sense."

Even though the act of suicide permanently alters the lives of those of us it leaves in its wake, some survivors come to regard their loved one's deaths as an understandable response to terminal suffering and despair. "It was only when I began to understand the level of pain my son must have been going through that I was able to accept what he did to himself and to me," explains Hannah, a sixty-six-year-old housewife who lives in a Los Angeles suburb. "My son shot himself five years ago, one month after his fortieth birthday. I had just assumed that he was happy: He had a wonderful wife, two lovely sons, and seemed content with his job. I have always prided myself on my sensitivity and intuition; looking back at that time, I can't believe I was so blind. How could I have not seen that my own son was in a terrible depression and contemplating suicide?

"He called me the night before he killed himself. It was a very strange conversation. My son told me that I was a survivor, that when everyone else fell down, I would remain standing. I had no idea what he was talking about. He also said that he had made some very poor decisions in his life and he was sorry. I was confused but reminded him that there are always chances for new beginnings, that he was only forty years old and would have endless opportunities to make changes in his life. He said he loved me and then we said goodnight. It was the last time I ever spoke to him.

"In retrospect, I now understand that my son was saying goodbye to me, even though he didn't give me the chance to say goodbye to him. The next day, he shot himself while out on his morning run. I was making breakfast when the phone rang. It was a policeman who said, and I quote, 'I'm sorry, but your son is no longer with us.' I had absolutely no idea what he was talking about. Had my son been spirited away like in some kind of science fiction movie? The policeman told me that my son had been found with the gun still in his mouth, but because he had died instantly there had been minimal pain. I still had no idea what this man was saying to me. He could have been speaking a foreign language, for all I knew.

"I was numb for a long, long time. Then, around one-and-a-half years after my son killed himself, I began to feel extremely depressed and suicidal. For the first time, I realized the level of mental anguish that my son must have been suffering when he took his life. Before that, I could only imagine what it was like; now I could identify with his state of mind. I said to myself, If this is how low my son was, the poor child had no choice but to end his life. At that moment, I decided to go ahead and kill myself. It was the only way I could think of to get myself out of my situation.

"I picked out an entrance on the freeway near my house where I planned to drive my car into the oncoming path of one of those huge tractor-trailers. Every time I passed that spot, I visualized the exact way my death would occur. These were not abstract thoughts; I was preparing my suicide very carefully.

"In the depths of my despair, the thought that I could end my life so easily and swiftly helped me immensely. One day, I actually found myself driving over to the entrance, ready to be crushed to death by the first truck that came by. Do you want to know what stopped me? I remembered what my son's death did to everyone, and I knew that no matter how awful I was feeling, I couldn't leave my grandchildren with the burden of my suicide. My son might not have had a choice, but I did.

"As I began to understand why my son wanted to die, I started to forgive him. Despondency is total blackness—you can't see through it and it pulls you down like a magnetic force. You have to fight not to go under with it. It breaks my heart to realize my son was so alone when he died. I just pray he has finally stopped hurting."

Although the idea of seeking an escape from our pain can help us make it through the darkness of the night, most of us, like Hannah, do not act on our fantasies of self-destruction. "A close friend of mine who had AIDS incorporated the possibility of suicide as part of his survival," relates Ben, a thirty-four-year-old fund-raiser from New York. "First, he said he would kill himself when his T-cells fell below a certain level. After they dropped to that number, he decided to wait to end his life until he got a Kaposi's lesion on his face. When this happened, he said he would hold out until he was down to a certain weight, then if he had to use a cane, then if he started to lose his sight, and so on.

"Everything happened as he feared. But as each condition for his planned suicide was met, he would set another goal that would allow him to keep living. It was as if there was this fixed distance between the horizon of his fear of dying and his desire to be in control of his destiny. Although he suffered terribly, he never did kill himself, dying, instead, when his life came to its end."

The French philosopher and novelist Albert Camus wrote in *The Myth of Sisyphus:* "There is but one truly serious philosophical problem and that is suicide. Judging whether life is or is not worth living amounts to answering the fundamental question of philosophy." Survivors not only must try to understand the reasons why our loved ones answered no to Camus's fundamental question of philosophy, we must also struggle to accept the fact that their decision to commit suicide will forever transform our lives.

"I believe that total forgiveness is almost impossible to achieve," says Carol, the Minneapolis magazine publisher whose husband drowned himself just weeks before the birth of their daughter. "After four years, I have come to believe that life moves on, no matter what happens or doesn't happen. The biggest step for me was to understand that Josh's suicide was an outgrowth of depression and possible mental illness; it was not a normal way of responding to stress. I have to assume that my husband did not know what he was doing when he decided to walk into the lake and drown himself. It is important for me to believe that people commit suicide to end their pain, not to create pain for others.

"Forgiving myself is an even slower process. I have gone over this a trillion times and what helps is realizing that clues are more apparent after the fact. Every book on suicide that I have read emphasizes that people who are hell-bent on killing themselves will accomplish it, no matter what you do. Sometimes I believe it, sometimes I don't. In addition, I have to forgive myself for being a less-than-perfect wife. I don't like failing, and even though I understand suicide was Josh's choice, I can't help feeling I'm also part of his failure.

"Recently, my daughter said to me, 'Why did you let

Daddy swim if he was tired?' I told her that I wasn't there, that I didn't know he was planning to go into the water. What I really felt like saying was 'I had nothing to do with your Daddy's death.' But do I really believe that? I know this is only the first of many similar conversations my daughter and I will be having on this subject. At times like these, I find it almost impossible to forgive Josh, because his suicide will always be a major factor in my relationship with my daughter. His decision to die will remain a complex, unresolved issue between us for the rest of our lives."

The suicide of a loved one reshapes us: Our beliefs and perceptions have been shaken by the deliberate, permanent departure of a person we have cared for, depended on, cherished, and nurtured. To the existential question of "Why?," our loved ones have answered, "Why not?" and have chosen to leave. We must deal not only with their irreversible decision but also with all the unfinished business they have left behind.

Survivors instinctively comprehend that in order to move on, we must not allow the disbelief, anger, and sorrow that follows suicide to define our lives. We must accept our loved one's deaths as self-inflicted and intentional; we have to struggle against becoming bitter and hard; we cannot permit our own feelings of despair to paralyze and eventually harm us.

"I knew I didn't want to be standing in front of Kim's grave, year after year, crying out, 'Why did you do this?' " says Valerie. "I refuse to choose the darkness—either for my daughter or for me."

At the conclusion of my first support meeting, one month after it seemed as if Harry's suicide had singed every layer of protective skin from my body, Jean-Claude asked us all to observe a minute of silence to remember our loved ones. He said that we should try to think of their pain along with our own. I understood that he was asking us to forgive them, to empathize with their suffering. I looked around at the others in the circle. Some had their eyes closed as if in deep reflection; others were crying openly. There were also several who stared straight ahead with the empty gaze of refugees from devastating earthquakes or war-torn lands, whose worlds have been ripped from under them for reasons they would never understand.

I knew that my eyes must be blazing. The fury I felt at Harry's abandonment had filled me with strength; my rage propelled me out of bed in the morning, arming me for the grueling struggle to restore order in my life. It was as if Harry and I had argued ferociously, and he had slammed the door in my face. I could plead with him to let me talk. I could beg. I could bang on the door until my hands were bloody. But he had spoken the last word and won the fight. How could he have done this to me?

Yet, as I felt the sorrow of the others in the group suffuse the stark yet safe space, I began to understand that it was not us, but Harry, and Kevin's father, and Hal's daughter, and Victoria's husband, and all the people we had loved who had lost the argument. We were shattered but would heal. We were frightened but had braved a bitter-cold winter evening to relive our nightmares with strangers who, like us, hungered to survive. We had years ahead of us to accept the knowledge that there were no victors in this battle, that there was no battle at all.

Suicide seems so senseless for those of us who have been left behind. I picture Harry swirling downward, losing the ability to reach out to anyone, even to see the hands that were stretching out to him. But can I forgive him for giving up? Should I absolve him of not trying hard enough? Yet, where was I during this time? Even when the medical examiner told me that there was no way of stopping death from occurring once the first drop of Thiopental had entered Harry's bloodstream, I knew my husband's lethal injection was only the last in many steps that had preceded it. Harry had researched the method of suicide he was planning to use for weeks before his death; he was imploding in front of my very eyes. How did I miss it? Why couldn't I stop it?

Survivors will always cry for the missed chance, for the waste of potential, for the hindsight that proves so illuminating now that it is too late. Harry and I could have had a full marriage, his healing touch might have saved many lives, he would have watched our dog grow old. I will always be filled with regret; I will always wish for a happy ending. But I am the keeper of Harry's memory, and so I must be whole. I must accept that I could not have stopped my husband from doing what he desired, that I could not have altered time. I have chosen to love again and laugh from my heart and enjoy the freedom of being alive. Just as Harry's decisions were his alone, I, too, have made my choice, and it is life, with all its unpredictable mysteries.

Have I forgiven Harry? I forgive him many times a day. And what about myself? When the pain of remorse assaults me, I remember that I loved my husband very much. I also remember Eduardo's wise advice: I turn around and walk away, but this time from my own guilt and shame. As I begin not only to move on but also to grow and flourish, I am aware I will be forgiving both my husband and myself continually for the rest of my life.

Part Five

AFTERWORD

16

Making Sense
of the Chaos

I am sitting in an elegant Japanese restaurant with two close
friends, both of whom are vibrantly attractive and sparkling
with energy. Over sushi, we engage in an impassioned discussion that lasts for several hours. "Can you imagine if someone
were listening in on this conversation?" one of us eventually
marvels. We explode with laughter. Because interspersed with
talk about careers and politics and family matters, we are recounting, once again, our old, familiar war stories. Although

we have heard one another's stories of survival after suicide many times before, we know that every retelling will uncover fresh insights, recovered details, and unexpected interpretations.

Police investigations, bloodied clothes, autopsy reports, crying bouts, panic attacks, crazy thoughts, missed opportunities, unanswered questions: We have integrated the remnants of our extraordinary ordeals into our new worlds. Seven years after we met at our first support group, we are as close as sisters. We comfortably move between the current issues that occupy our time and the singular event that links us. We speak freely and openly about our husband, our daughter, our mother, constantly repeating ourselves without fear of being judged or censured.

Like every other person who has lost a loved one to suicide, my friends and I have been transported to the realm of philosophers and poets and religious thinkers. We now find ourselves reflecting on the mystery and power of the will to survive, deliberating the meaning of human existence as we go about our daily lives.

Over the past years, I have been on a journey that was not of my choosing. During this time, I have tried to comprehend the reason my husband elected to embrace the darkness, while I struggled to sustain the light. Why did Harry decide to join the unknown monster lurking in the closet, the one who has haunted us since we were little children afraid of the night? How have I—and all the remarkable people I have met during my travels—willed ourselves to pick up the pieces of our shattered lives, to rebuild and, eventually, to rejoice?

Each person I have interviewed for this book speaks of a singular bond among suicide survivors that pierces through our isolation and fear. Unlike our loved ones, whose pain was so enveloping that they were unable to hear our shouts of help, we refuse to be exiled by despair. As we reach out to others, we discover inner strengths we never knew existed. Although we did not ask for this test of our endurance—and would reverse the circumstances if given the choice—we discover that we are more resilient, less afraid, more empathetic and understanding as a result of what has happened to us.

On an ordinary December morning seven years ago, I began an odyssey that would lead me to confront the very question of mortality. I was forced to look inside myself and decide whether I wanted to continue living or join my husband in his black abyss. I will never understand my rationale for moving on, as I will never know why Harry chose to let go. Yet, despite my initial shock and confusion, I instinctively understood that by losing faith and abandoning hope, I would be validating the suicide of my husband.

"Our lives are like books that have been scorched in a fire," says Emmy, the physician's assistant from Santa Fe whose fourteen-year-old son shot himself five years ago. "At first, we think the book has been totally burned. But then we pick it up and see that even though some pages are missing, others are still intact. This is the survivor's story. We have to fill in that part of our life that has been destroyed and taken away, both for ourselves and for the people we have lost."

Many courageous people revealed the personal and painful details of their experiences to me to help diminish the stigma associated with suicide. These men and women have prevailed in the face of unthinkable events, preferring to risk new beginnings than succumb to seemingly inevitable endings. Like them, as I have surrendered the secrecy that so defined my life after Harry's suicide, I have been able to reclaim my own sense of self, apart and distinct from my husband's decision to die.

In a journey filled with unfamiliar landmarks and unexpected turns, those of us whose loved ones have ended their lives so abruptly and with such anguish do not waver from one unassailable certainty: We dearly miss our mothers and sisters, our husbands and daughters, our brothers and sons, our wives and fathers, our relatives and friends. Yet, our survival—and even triumph—is the legacy we now carry forward, a testament to the memory of those we have loved and inexplicably lost.

Part Six

RESOURCES

17

Organizations and Resource Material

The following list includes national organizations involved with issues of concern to suicide survivors. These groups offer a variety of resource material related to suicide, including newsletters and pamphlets, and sponsor conferences and workshops for people who have lost a loved one to suicide.

1. American Association of Suicidology
   4201 Connecticut Ave., N.W., Suite 310
   Washington, DC 20008
   202-237-2280

A not-for-profit organization founded in 1968, the American Association of Suicidology (AAS) promotes research, public awareness programs, and education and training for professionals and volunteers with the goal of understanding and preventing suicide. AAS includes a division for survivors, which publishes a quarterly newsletter, a directory of survivor support groups throughout the United States and Canada, and a bibliography of books, pamphlets, articles, and other literature related to surviving the suicide of a loved one and suicide prevention. AAS also sponsors an annual conference, "Healing After Suicide," for people who have lost a loved one to suicide.

2. Friends for Survival, Inc.
   P.O. Box 214463
   Sacramento, CA 95821
   916-392-0664 (Office)
   800-646-7322 (Suicide Loss Helpline)

Organized by and for survivors, Friends for Survival is a not-for-profit peer support group that provides direct services at no cost to those who have lost a loved one to suicide. The group offers the following services: a monthly newsletter; information and referrals regarding local support groups; list of printed resources and tapes; the toll-free Suicide Loss Helpline, staffed by volunteers who have experienced the suicide of a loved one; conferences and retreats; and information on forming survivor support groups.

3. American Suicide Foundation
   1045 Park Avenue
   New York, NY 10028
   212-410-1111

This nonprofit organization funds research, education, and treatment programs to prevent suicide and also offers outreach to suicide survivors through its newsletter, referral service, and conferences.

4. Heartbeat
   2015 Devon St.
   Colorado Springs, CO 80909
   719-596-2575

A mutual-support organization for those who have lost a loved one to suicide, Heartbeat provides information on starting local survivor support groups and referrals to support groups throughout the country.

5. SPAN (Suicide Prevention Advocacy Network)
   5034 Odins Way
   Marietta, GA 30068
   770-998-8819

A cooperative, community-based advocacy group, SPAN consists of survivors of suicide committed to reducing the incidence of suicide in the United States.

6. Ray of Hope
   P.O. Box 2323
   Iowa City, IA 52244
   319-337-9890

A nonprofit organization for families and friends of people who have lost a loved one to suicide, Ray of Hope provides information on resource material related to suicide and starting support groups for survivors.

7. The Link Counseling Center
   348 Mt. Vernon Highway, N.E.
   Atlanta, GA 30328
   404-256-9797

This nonprofit counseling center offers a Suicide Prevention Outreach Aftercare and Resources program that provides training for developing community-based suicide survivor support teams throughout the country. The group also offers resource material for suicide survivors.

Additional resources of interest to survivors of suicide include:

1. "Grief After Suicide," a pamphlet published by the Mental Health Association in Waukesha County, Inc., 2220 Silvernail Rd., Pewaukee, WI 53072, tel. 414-547-9136 (50 cents each).

2. "Facts for Families," a series of pamphlets describing the warning signs of youth depression and suicide, published by the American Academy of Child and Adolescent Psychiatry, P.O. Box 96106, Washington, DC 20090, tel. 800-333-7636.

3. Numerous resource material regarding suicide and suicide prevention, including "Suicide in the United States, 1980–1992" and "Youth Suicide Prevention Programs: A Resource Guide," can be obtained free of charge from the Centers for Disease Control and Pre-

vention, 4770 Buford Highway, K60, Atlanta, GA 30341, tel. 770-488-4677.

4. Current statistics and other material related to suicide are available at no cost from the National Institute of Mental Health, 5600 Fishers Lane, Rockville, MD 20857, tel. 301-443-4513.

5. Pamphlets and other literature on bereavement are available from the Association for Death Education and Counseling, 638 Prospect Ave., Hartford, CT 06105, tel. 203-586-7503.

6. The suicide survivors mailing list on the Internet provides an electronic support group for people who have lost a loved one to suicide. To subscribe, send mail to: listserve@research.canon.oz.au containing: subscribe suicide-survivors, your name in the body of the message.

Support Groups
for Survivors

Support groups for suicide survivors are located throughout
the United States and Canada. The following list includes
the names and telephone numbers of peer support groups that
are available free of charge, arranged by geographical loca-
tion. These groups are organized on a community, grassroots
level and are not affiliated with a specific association or organization. Additional information on survivor groups can also
be obtained from the following sources.

- The American Association of Suicidology (AAS) provides referrals to local support groups throughout the United States and Canada and also publishes a comprehensive directory of survivors-of-suicide support groups. Tel. 202-237-2280.

- The American Suicide Foundation offers a free national referral service that provides local listings for support groups throughout the United States. Tel. 800-273-4042.

- Friends for Survival, Inc. provides information about local support groups in the United States and Canada on its toll-free Suicide Loss Helpline. Tel. 800-646-7322.

- Heartbeat refers suicide survivors to support groups in their areas. Tel. 719-596-2575.

- Local mental health community centers and crisis hotlines often have information on support groups for suicide survivors in their communities.

UNITED STATES

Alabama

> Birmingham: Crisis Center, Inc. 205-323-7782
> Florence: Day-By-Day. 205-766-9161

Alaska

> Anchorage: Support Group for Suicide Survivors.
>   907-272-3100
> Fairbanks: Fairbanks Crisis Line. 907-451-8600

Arizona

Tempe: Survivors of Suicide. 602-784-1514
Yuma: Survivors of Suicide. 520-783-1860

Arkansas

Little Rock: Survivors of Suicide, Arkansas Chapter.
501-337-1930

California

Berkeley: Survivors of Suicide. 510-889-1104
Burlingame: Survivors of Suicide. 415-692-6662
Castro Valley: Survivors of Suicide. 510-889-1104
Chico: Suicide Survivors Bereavement Support Group.
916-891-2832
Davis: Friends and Families of Suicide Loss.
916-756-7542
Fresno: Fresno Survivors of Suicide Loss. 800-822-8448;
209-435-7669
Garden Grove: Survivors of Suicide. 714-971-4032
Jackson: New Horizons. 209-223-0793
Modesto: Survivors of Suicide. 209-577-0615
Napa/Solano: Survivors of Suicide. 707-252-6222
Pacific Grove: Loving Outreach for Survivors.
408-375-6966
Redding: Suicide Survivors Support Group.
916-225-5252
Redlands/San Bernadino: Survivors of Suicide Support
Group. 909-792-4862
Sacramento: Friends for Survival. 916-392-0664
San Diego: Survivors of Suicide. 619-482-0297
San Francisco: Self Help Grief Group. 415-750-5355

San Luis Obispo: Suicide Survivors Group.
805-544-2266
Santa Barbara: Suicide Survivors. 805-965-5555
Santa Rosa: Survivors of Suicide. 707-542-5045
Upland: Hope After Suicide. 909-982-7534
Vacaville: Bay Area Survivors of Suicide. 707-452-8520
Walnut Creek: Survivors of Suicide. 510-944-0645

Colorado

Arvada: Heartbeat. 303-424-4094
Boulder: Heartbeat. 303-444-3496
Colorado Springs: Heartbeat. 719-596-2575
Denver: Heartbeat. 303-934-8464
Denver: Parents of Suicides. 303-322-7450
Denver: Survivors Group. 303-766-3328
Florence: Heartbeat. 719-269-2140
Ft. Collins: Suicide Resource Center of Larimer County.
970-635-9301
Grand Junction: Heartbeat. 970-243-2467
Greeley: Suicide Education and Support Services.
970-353-0639
Littleton: Heartbeat. 303-794-3564
Pueblo: Heartbeat. 719-564-6642

Connecticut

Hartford: Safe Place/The Samaritans of the Capital Re-
gion. 203-232-2121
Middletown: Survivors of Suicide. 203-343-5814;
203-347-4003
Southbury: Survivors of Suicide. 203-264-5613
Wethersfield: Suicide Bereavement. 203-563-3035

Delaware

Millsboro: Survivors of Suicide. 800-287-6423
Wilmington: Survivors of Suicide. 302-656-8308

District of Columbia

There are no groups currently in Washington, DC.

Florida

Altamonte Springs: Survivors of Suicide Support Group.
   407-869-9617
Boca Raton: Suicide Survivors Support Group.
   407-394-7979
Bradenton: Hospice of SW Florida. 941-739-8940
Cape Coral: Survivors of Suicide. 941-945-0338
Daytona Beach: Assure. 904-252-5785; 904-756-3198
Ft. Lauderdale: Survivors of Suicide. 305-467-6333
Jacksonville: Self Help Support Group. 904-721-4282
Lauderhill: Suicide Survivors Support Group.
   954-968-6795; 954-768-0434
Miami: Suicide Survivors Support Group. 305-653-1023
Palm Beach: The Courage to Survive. 407-747-3165
Pensacola: Survivors of Suicide. 904-438-9879
Pinellas Park: Survivors and Victims, United.
   813-791-3131
Rockledge: Crisis Services of Brevard, Inc. 407-631-8944

Georgia

Albany: Suicide Survivors. 912-883-1281
Atlanta: Bereavement Support Group. 404-505-7703;
   404-758-1329

Atlanta: Survivors of Suicide, Sandy Springs Chapter.
    404-256-9797
Douglas County: Survivors of Suicide. 770-432-1621,
    ext. 522; 770-436-4090
Henry County: Survivors of Suicide. 770-914-0626
Lawrenceville: Survivors of Suicide. 404-256-9797
Marietta: Survivors of Suicide, East Cobb Chapter.
    770-998-8819
Riverdale: Survivors of Suicide, Riverdale Chapter.
    770-998-8819
Roswell: Survivors of Suicide. 770-993-6218

Hawaii

Honolulu: Survivors of Suicide. 808-521-4555

Idaho

Boise: Survivors of Suicide. 208-338-1017; 208-345-2350
Idaho Falls: Survivors of Suicide. 208-522-0033

Illinois

Aurora: Survivors of Suicide. 708-897-5522
Chicago: LOSS: Loving Outreach to Survivors of Sui-
    cide. 312-655-7283; 312-655-7285
Decatur: Listening, Sharing, Caring (LSC).
    217-767-2268
Edgemont: Survivors of Suicide. 618-397-0963
Oak Brook: Compassionate Friends. 708-990-0010
Peoria: Survivors of Suicide. 309-693-5281;
    309-697-3342
Wood River: The C.O.-H.E.A.R.T.S. 618-251-4073

Indiana

Bloomington: SOS/Heartbeat. 812-334-3801
Columbus: Survivors of Suicide. 812-546-5820
Elkhart: Survivors of Suicide. 219-295-8156
Ft. Wayne: We the Living. 219-422-6402; 219-432-6293
Lafayette: Survivors of Suicide Support Group.
    317-742-0460

Iowa

Cedar Falls: Suicide Grief Support Group. 319-277-5369
Cedar Rapids: Suicide Survivors Group. 319-362-2174
Iowa City: Ray of Hope. 319-337-9890

Kansas

Topeka: Survivors of Suicide. 913-267-4547

Kentucky

Louisville: Survivors of Suicide. 502-589-4313
Middlesboro: Survivors of Suicide. 606-248-1678
Owensboro: Survivors of Suicide. 502-926-7565

Louisiana

Baton Rouge: Survivors of Suicide. 504-924-1431;
    504-924-3900
Monroe: Support After Suicide. 318-323-9479
New Orleans: Coping with Suicide. 504-834-1354

Maine

Portland: Survivors of Suicide. 207-871-4226
Rumford: Survivors of Suicide. 207-364-2651

Maryland

Baltimore: SEASONS: Suicide Bereavement.
410-882-2937
Bethesda: SEASONS: Suicide Bereavement.
301-460-4677
Crofton: Growing Through Grief. 410-721-0899
Westminster: SEASONS: Suicide Bereavement.
410-876-1047

Massachusetts

Andover: Safe Place/The Samaritans of Merrimack Valley. 508-688-6607
Boston: Safe Place/The Samaritans of Boston.
617-536-2460
Fall River: Safe Place/The Samaritans of Fall River/New Bedford. 508-673-3777; 508-999-7267
Falmouth: Safe Place/The Samaritans of Cape Cod.
508-548-8900
Framingham: Safe Place/The Samaritans of Suburban West. 508-875-4500
West Springfield: Survivors of Suicide. 413-734-9139

Michigan

Adrian: Survivors of Suicide. 517-263-7882
Cadillac: Survivors of Suicide. 616-826-3865
Detroit: Survivors of Suicide. 313-224-7000

East Lansing: Survivors of Suicide. 517-626-6317

Flint: Survivors of Suicide. 810-232-9950

Grand Rapids: West Michigan Survivors of Suicide.
      616-281-2058

Jackson: Survivors of Suicide. 517-783-2648

Kalamazoo: Survivors of Suicide. 616-381-4357

Lansing: Survivors of Suicide. 517-339-1529

Ludington: West Shore Survivors of Suicide.
      616-845-6854

Marquette: Survivors of Suicide. 906-228-3040

Port Huron: Survivors of Suicide. 810-794-4982

Saginaw: Survivors of Suicide. 517-781-0410

Spring Lake: West Michigan Survivors of Suicide.
      616-874-6439

Troy: Survivors of Suicide. 810-680-0796

Warren: Survivors of Suicide. 810-307-9100

Minnesota

Duluth: Suicide Survivors Support Group. 218-726-4402

Minneapolis: SAVE. 612-946-7998

St. Paul: Survivors of Suicide. 612-776-1565

Willmar: Support Group for Survivors of Suicide.
      612-235-5411

Mississippi

Jackson: Survivors of Suicide. 601-360-0814

Missouri

Springfield: Survivors of Suicide Group. 417-865-5943

St. Louis: Survivors of Suicide Support Group.
      314-647-3100

Montana

Missoula: Surviving Friends. 406-543-6132

Nebraska

Hastings: Heartbeat. 402-463-7804
Lincoln: Ray of Hope Survivors of Suicide.
  402-488-3827
Omaha: Survivors of Suicide Omaha. 402-558-4616

Nevada

Reno: Survivors of Suicide. 702-323-4533

New Hampshire

Derry: Coping with a Loved One's Suicide.
  603-329-5276
Exeter: Suicide Support. 603-778-7391
Keene: Safe Place/The Samaritans of Keene.
  603-357-5505
Manchester: Survivors of Suicide. 603-644-2525

New Jersey

Dumont: Survivors After Suicide. 201-385-4400
Madison: Survivors of Suicide. 201-786-5178
Piscataway: Survivors of Suicide. 908-235-4109
Toms River: Survivors of Suicide. 908-505-5437

New Mexico

Albuquerque: Survivors of Suicide. 505-858-1240

New York

Albany: Safe Place/The Samaritans of the Capital Dis-
   trict. 518-459-0196
Babylon: Compassionate Friends/Parents of Suicide.
   516-661-7012
Brooklyn: Ray of Hope. 718-738-9217
Buffalo: Suicide Bereavement Group. 716-685-2733
Douglaston (Queens): Survivors of Suicide Support
   Group. 516-466-8423
Flushing (Queens): Survivors of Suicide. 718-463-1639
Ithaca: After Suicide Support Group. 607-272-1505;
   607-272-1616
Massapequa: South Shore Suicide Survivors Group.
   516-798-7881
New York City (Manhattan): Safe Place/The Samaritans
   of New York. 212-673-3000
Port Jefferson: Survivors of Suicide. 516-474-6061
Rochester: After Suicide. 716-654-7262
Roslyn Heights: Survivors After the Suicide of a Loved
   One. 516-626-1971
Staten Island: Survivors of Suicide. 718-448-3306
White Plains: C.A.R.E.S. (for children and their fami-
   lies). 914-997-5849

North Carolina

Mount Airy: Survivors of Suicide. 910-789-5108

North Dakota

Bismark: Grief After Suicide. 800-472-2911;
   701-255-3692
Fargo: Suicide Survivor Support Group. 701-293-6462

Grand Forks: Survivors of Suicide. 701-795-3000
Minot: Survivors of Suicide. 701-857-2230
Wahpeton: Suicide Survivor Support Group.
    701-293-6462.

Ohio

Akron: Survivors. 216-253-9388
Canton: Survivors of Suicide. 216-452-6000
Cincinnati: Survivors After Suicide. 513-385-6110
Cincinnati: Survivors of Suicide (for children and their
    families). 513-841-1012
Columbus: Survivors of Suicide. 614-279-9382
Dayton: Survivors of Suicide. 513-297-9096
Delaware: Helpline. 800-684-2324
Lakewood: Survivors of Suicide. 216-521-1335
Toledo: Survivors of Suicide. 419-385-9205
Westerville: Survivors of Suicide. 614-882-9338
Youngstown: Survivors of Suicide Support Group.
    216-747-5111

Oklahoma

Norman: Survivors of Suicide. 405-329-4280
Oklahoma City: Survivors of Suicide. 405-942-1345
Tulsa: Survivors of Suicide. 918-585-1213

Oregon

Albany: Survivors of Suicide Support Group.
    503-394-3707
Medford: Healing from Suicide. 503-772-2527

Portland: The Dougy Center (for children and their families). 503-775-5683

Portland: Suicide Bereavement Support. 503-235-0476

Pennsylvania

Altoona: Support Group for Those Who Have Lost a Loved One Through Suicide. 814-946-2209

Butler: Survivors of Suicide. 412-287-1965

Fort Washington: Survivors of Suicide. 215-545-2242

Lancaster: Survivors of Suicide. 717-898-8239

Langhorne: Survivors of Suicide. 215-545-2242

Levittown: Survivors of Suicide. 215-545-2242

Lewisburg: Survivors of Suicide. 717-523-7509

Monaca: Suicide's Other Victims. 412-775-4165

Philadelphia: Survivors of Suicide. 215-545-2242

Philadelphia: Survivors of Suicide. 215-745-8247

Pittsburgh: Survivors of Suicide. 412-624-5170

Quakertown: Survivors of Suicide. 215-536-5143

Wilkes-Barre: Survivors of Suicide. 717-822-7118

Rhode Island

Providence: Safe Place/The Samaritans of Rhode Island. 401-272-4044

South Carolina

Anderson: Survivors of Suicide. 864-646-5167

Charleston: Survivors of Suicide. 803-744-4357

Columbia: Survivors of Suicide. 803-356-2874

Greenville: Survivors of Suicide Support Group. 864-271-8888

South Dakota

Sioux Falls: Survivors of Suicide. 605-336-1974

Tennessee

Chattanooga: Living After Suicide. 423-875-2509
Nashville: Survivors of Suicide Support Group.
   615-244-7444

Texas

Amarillo: Surviving Connection. 806-342-3600
Corpus Christi: Survivors After Suicide. 512-853-1964
Dallas: Survivors of Suicide Support Group.
   214-828-1000
Ft. Worth: Survivors of Suicide. 817-654-5343
Houston: Survivors of Suicide. 713-228-1505
Lubbock: Survivors of Suicide. 806-765-7272
Lufkin: Survivors of Suicide. 409-632-1514
Midland: Survivors of Suicide Support Group.
   915-685-1566
Plano: Survivors of Suicide. 214-881-0088
San Angelo: Heartbeat. 915-944-1666
San Antonio: S.O.L.O.S. 210-695-9136

Utah

Layton: Legacy. 801-771-8476
Park City: SEASONS: Suicide Bereavement.
   801-649-8327

Vermont

There are no groups currently in the state of Vermont.

Virginia

Falls Church: Suicide Survivors Support Group.
   703-273-3454; 703-866-2100
Hopewell: Healing After Suicide. 804-458-3895
Newport News: Survivors of Suicide Support Group.
   757-875-0060
Portsmouth: Survivors of Suicide Support Group.
   804-483-5111
Richmond: Surviving. 804-780-6911
Virginia Beach: Survivors of Suicide. 757-469-6000
Winchester: Survivors of Suicide Support Group.
   540-667-1178

Washington

Auburn: Survivors of Suicide. 206-833-7127
Kennewick: Survivors of Suicide. 509-783-7416
Seattle: Survivors of Suicide. 206-461-3222
Seattle: Survivors of Suicide. 206-772-5141
Spokane: Survivors of a Loved One's Suicide.
   509-483-3310
Tacoma: Survivors of Suicide. 206-474-3330

West Virginia

Huntington: Heartbeat. 304-526-6001
Wheeling: Survivors of Suicide Support Group.
   304-277-3916

Wisconsin

Appleton: Fox Valley Survivors of Suicide. 414-739-1231
Eau Claire: Suicide Survivors Support Group.
715-833-6028
La Crosse: Karis Support Group. 608-785-0530, ext.
3652
Madison: Survivors of Suicide. 608-251-2345
Marshfield: Survivors of Suicide. 715-387-7753
Milwaukee: Survivors Helping Survivors. 414-649-6000,
ext. 6230
Sheboygan: Suicide Loss Support Group. 414-458-3951
Wisconsin Rapids: Survivors of Suicide. 715-421-1942

Wyoming

Cheyenne: Share and Care. 307-637-3753

CANADA

Alberta

Calgary: Canadian Mental Health Association Suicide
Services. 403-297-1744
Calgary: Fellowship of Suicide Survivors. 403-283-6812;
403-228-7943
Edmonton: The Support Network—Suicide Bereavement
Support Group. 403-482-0198
Ft. McMurray: Some Other Solutions Society for Crisis
Prevention. 403-743-8605

British Columbia

Nanaimo: Survivors of Suicide. 604-758-3190
Vancouver: S.A.F.E.R. 604-879-9251

Nova Scotia

Springhill: Springhill Ray of Hope. 902-597-3611

Ontario

Hamilton: Telecare of Hamilton. 905-525-8611
London: Suicide Bereavement Support Group.
519-434-9191
Toronto: Suicide Support Program. 416-595-1716
Windsor: Suicide Bereavement. 519-255-7440

Quebec

Montreal: Suicide-Action Montreal. 514-723-4000
Quebec: Centre de Prevention du Suicide, CPS.
418-683-4588
Saguenay–Lac-St-Jean: Centre de Prevention du Suicide
02. 418-545-1919

 **19**

Bibliography

Books

Alexander, V. *Words I Never Thought to Speak: Stories of Life in the Wake of Suicide.* Lexington Press, 1991.

Blumenthal, Susan, and Kupfer, David (eds.). *Suicide Over the Life Cycle: Risk Factors Assessment and Treatment of Suicidal Patients.* American Psychiatric Association, 1990.

Bolton, Iris, with Mitchell, Curtis. *My Son, My Son: A Guide to Healing After a Suicide in the Family.* Bolton Press, 1984.

Clark, D.C. (ed.). *Clergy Response to Suicidal Persons and Their Family Members.* Exploration Press, 1993.

Diagnostic and Statistical Manual of Mental Disorders (Third Edition, Revised). American Psychiatric Association, 1987.

Dunne, Edward, John McIntosh and Karen Dunne-Maxim (eds.). *Suicide and Its Aftermath: Understanding and Counseling the Survivors.* W.W. Norton & Company, 1987.

Finkbeiner, Ann. *After the Death of a Child: Living with Loss Through the Years.* The Free Press, 1996.

Freud, E.L. (ed.). *The Letters of Sigmund Freud.* McGraw-Hill, 1960.

Graves, Edward (ed.). *McGill's Life Insurance.* The American College, 1994.

Hartley, Mariette. *Breaking the Silence.* G.P. Putnam's Son, 1990.

Hendin, Herbert. *Suicide in America.* W.W. Norton & Company, 1995.

Lamm, Maurice. *The Jewish Way in Death and Mourning.* Jonathan David Publishers, Inc., 1969.

Leenaars, A. (ed.). *Suicidology: Essays in Honor of Edwin Shneidman.* Jason Aronson, 1993.

Lockridge, Larry. *Shade of the Raintree: The Life and Death of Ross Lockridge, Jr.* Penguin Books, 1995.

Lukas, Christopher and Seiden, Henry. *Silent Grief: Living in the Wake of Suicide.* Charles Scribner's Sons, 1988.

Miller, John (ed.). *On Suicide: Great Writers on the Ultimate Question.* Chronicle Books, 1992.

Osterweis, Marian, and Townsend, Jessica. *Health Professionals and the Bereaved.* National Institute of Mental Health, 1988.

Slaby, Andrew, and Garfinkel, Lili Frank. *No One Saw My Pain: Why Teens Kill Themselves.* W.W. Norton & Company, 1994.

Vanderbilt, Gloria. *A Mother's Story.* Alfred A. Knopf, 1996.

Wolman, Benjamin (ed.). *Between Survival and Suicide.* Gardner Press, Inc., 1976.

Periodicals

"Dual Effects from the Holocaust Found in Survivors' Children," *The New York Times,* August 9, 1979.

"Elderly Suicide Rate Is up 9% over 12 Years," *The New York Times*, January 4, 1996.

Gorkin, M. "On the Suicide of One's Patient," *Bulletin of the Menninger Clinic*, 1985.

"Grief After Suicide," Mental Health Association in Waukesha County, 1981.

Hendin, Herbert, and Klerman, Gerald. "Physician-assisted Suicide: The Dangers of Legalization," *American Journal of Psychiatry*, January 1993.

Kachur, S.P., et al. "Suicide in the United States, 1980–1992," Centers for Disease Control and Prevention, National Center for Injury Prevention and Control, 1995.

Kellermann, Arthur, et al. "Suicide in the Home in Relation to Gun Ownership," *The New England Journal of Medicine*, August 13, 1992.

Marzuk, Peter, Kenneth Tardiff and Charles Hirsch. "The Epidemiology of Murder-Suicide," *Journal of the American Medical Association*, June 17, 1992.

"The Mystery of Suicide," *Newsweek*, April 18, 1994.

Ness, David, and Pfeffer, Cynthia. "Sequelae of Bereavement Resulting from Suicide," *American Journal of Psychiatry*, March 1990.

"No Bones About New Home Law," New York *Daily News*, August 11, 1995.

"Pataki Weighs Bill on Sale of Houses with Pasts," *The New York Times*, June 28, 1995.

"Review and Outlook: Self-Fulfilling Prophesy" [Editorial], *The Wall Street Journal*, July 28, 1993.

Shaffer, David, Veronica Vieland, Ann Garland, Mary Roja, Maureen Underwood, and Carey Busner. "Adolescent Suicide Attempters: Response to Suicide-Prevention Programs," *Journal of the American Medical Association*, December 26, 1990.

"Suicide—What Can Be Done?" [Editorial], *The New England Journal of Medicine*, August 13, 1992.

Tabor, Mary. "Publishing," *The New York Times*, April 3, 1995.

Taff, Mark, and Boglioli, Lauren. "Minister's Death Suggests Car Crash as Suicide," *The New York Times*, April 6, 1995.

"Teen Suicide," American Academy of Child and Adolescent Psychiatry, 1995.

"Youth Suicide Prevention Programs: A Resource Guide," Centers for Disease Control and Prevention, 1992.

"Youth Suicide: The Physician's Role in Suicide Prevention" [Editorial], *Journal of the American Medical Association*, December 26, 1990.